How the BEST TEACHERS Differentiate Instruction

Elizabeth Breaux
and
Monique Boutte Magee

EYE ON EDUCATION
6 DEPOT WAY WEST, SUITE 106
LARCHMONT, NY 10538
(914) 833-0551
(914) 833-0761 fax
www.eyeoneducation.com

A sincere effort has been made to supply the identity of those who have created specific strategies. Any omissions have been unintentional.

Library of Congress Cataloging-in-Publication Data

Breaux, Elizabeth, 1961-

How the best teachers differentiate instruction / Elizabeth Breaux and Monique Boutte Magee.

p. cm.

Includes bibliographical references.

ISBN 978-1-59667-140-9

1. Effective teaching--United States. 2. Learning. 3. Educational innovations--United States. 4. Educational change--United States. I. Magee, Boutte. II. Title.

LB1775.2.B74 2010

371.39'4--dc22

2009044000

10 9 8 7 6 5 4 3 2

Also Available from EYE ON EDUCATION

How the BEST TEACHERS
Avoid the 20 Most Common Teaching Mistakes
Elizabeth Breaux

Classroom Management Simplified!
Elizabeth Breaux

How to Reach and Teach ALL Students—Simplified!
Elizabeth Breaux

REAL Teachers, REAL Challenges, REAL Solutions:
25 Ways to Handle the Challenges of the Classroom Effectively
Annette and Elizabeth Breaux

Differentiated by Readiness: Strategies and Lesson Plans
for Tiered Instruction Grade K-8
Joni Turville, Linda Allen, and LeAnn Nichelsen

Differentiating by Student Interest: Strategies & Lesson Plans
Joni Turville

Differentiating by Student Preferences: Strategies & Lesson Plans
Joni Turville

Differentiated Instruction: A Guide for Elementary School Teachers
Amy Benjamin

Differentiated Instruction for K-8 Math and Science:
Activities and Lesson Plans
Mary Hamm and Dennis Adams

50 Ways to Improve Student Behavior:
Simple Solutions to Complex Challenges
Annette L. Breaux and Todd Whitaker

101 Answers for New Teachers and Their Mentors:
Effective Teaching Tips for Daily Classroom Use
Annette L. Breaux

Seven Simple Secrets:
What the Best Teachers Know and Do!
Annette L. Breaux and Todd Whitaker

Dedication

To Madison, Bailee, and Simone...
May each teacher you encounter on your journey
nurture your individualities,
and teach you as they would their own.

About the Authors

Elizabeth Breaux is one of the most practical, down-to-earth, informative, and entertaining authors and speakers in education today. She has spoken to audiences across the country. She leaves them laughing, crying, and certain that they have chosen the right profession—teaching. She is the author of *Classroom Management—SIMPLIFIED*; *How to Reach and Teach ALL Students SIMPLIFIED*; *How the BEST TEACHERS Avoid the 20 Most Common Teaching Mistakes*; and the co-author, with her sister Annette Breaux, of *Real Teachers, Real Challenges, Real Solutions.*

A former curriculum coordinator and classroom teacher, she currently trains and supports new teachers in Lafayette, LA. Also, she is one of the coordinators of TIPS, an induction program for new teachers in Lafayette, LA. In addition, she trains assessors for the Louisiana Department of Education and is an international presenter for the Bureau of Education and Research.

Liz has taught and worked with at-risk students for 25 years and believes that there is not a more challenging and rewarding job in the world. Her message has always been a simple one: "I cannot teach my students until I reach my students."

Monique Boutte Magee is an innovative, practical, "think-out-of-the-box" middle school administrator. She is currently the principal at Lafayette Middle School in Lafayette, LA, and has served as an administrator for eight years in the public school system.

Monique has assisted her teachers in transitioning from the traditional methods of instructing to the differentiated, tech-savvy, modern age of teaching. Because she keeps abreast of the current trends and best practices in education through the use of a data-driven curriculum coupled with modern "new practices" in education, she has assisted her teachers in improving standardized test scores and the school's annual yearly performance by 18 points in 5 years.

Monique has been an educator for 15 years and has worked with all types of learners. She believes all children can learn given the motivation, the appropriate curriculum, innovative teaching techniques, and an impeccable teacher.

Monique became an educator to make a difference in the lives of children and has made a difference in the lives of many. Monique's message is as practical as it is heartfelt: "Teach and treat all children as though they were your own."

Foreword

It is the quality of the teacher that is the key to the educational success of the student. It is not new textbooks, innovative teaching techniques, or state-of-the-art facilities that make up the bottom line but rather we, the teachers. Without quality teachers, the most innovative and well-intended advances in education are stopped in their tracks.

We truly make the difference in the lives of every student we teach. In the hands of a quality teacher, all of the above-mentioned are priceless. In the hands of an ineffective teacher, they are worthless... mere "things" that serve only to mask the fact that no transfer of knowledge is occurring. Education cannot occur in the absence of excellence that comes in the form of a superior teacher.

We firmly believe that we carry the awesome responsibility of being in perpetual search of excellence and that we must never lose our focus on the fact that each child, each human, is different. We must vow to reach our students and to teach our students using the methods that best suit the needs of the individual.

This book will provide you with the tools to do just that. You do not need more programs, newer textbooks, or nicer facilities to become a better teacher. You simply need a strong will and a few straightforward, practical, doable, easily implemented methods and strategies that will foster interest and growth in every child you teach. Their educations are in your hands... and now, here within the pages of this book, are the tools. We hope that you will find them as effective and as effortless to implement as we have and that your students will begin to wonder why the time flies so quickly in your classroom! Best wishes!

Table of Contents

Free Downloads

A large selection of the figures, templates and tools in the book are also available on Eye On Education's web site: www.eyeoneducation.com. Book buyers have been granted permission to print out these Adobe Acrobat© documents and duplicate them to distribute to your students.

You can access these downloads by visiting Eye On Education's website: www.eyeoneducation.com. Click on FREE Downloads or search or browse our website to find this book and then scroll down for downloading instructions. You'll need your bookbuyer access code: **DBM-7140-9**

Introduction

I am me, I am not you
I can hear you when you speak
I listen, but I do not understand
If I cannot understand today, and could not understand yesterday
I will not understand tomorrow
You can say it again and again, over and over
The same old way
But it means nothing
I do not disrespect you; I simply do not understand you.

When you show me, the picture becomes clearer
Like a light illuminating a darkened room
Where before I was scared and lost
The picture is familiar, and I feel that I have been there
I am able to connect and would like to see more.

When you allow me to do it, I understand
It makes sense, so I embrace it
You assist me at first, but I am comfortable when set free
I will not quit, because now I am involved
I yearn to do more
Please allow me, and
I will show you that I can learn...

—Elizabeth Breaux,
from *How to Reach and Teach*
ALL Students—SIMPLIFIED

What We've Learned about Teaching

- We've learned that a quality teacher can change the life of a student.
- We've learned that teaching is hard, but extremely rewarding, work.
- We've learned that students will not learn from someone whom they do not respect.
- We've learned that adults do not learn from someone whom they do not respect.
- We've learned that "busy work" is often created to keep the teacher from being busy.
- We've learned that we learn by doing.
- We've learned that when children are bored, they are not learning.
- We've learned that when children cannot relate, they do not engage.
- We've learned that each child is a unique individual with distinctive needs, interests, and Learning Styles.
- We've learned that we must be in continuous search of excellence.
- We've learned that teaching is a privilege…one that we must never take lightly….

What This Book Will Do for You

- If you want to take charge of instruction and achievement in your classroom,
- If you want to create a calm, caring, structured, and stress-free learning environment,
- If you want to truly make a difference in the life of every student who walks into your classroom,
- If you want the techniques that will help you to help your students achieve optimal learning success,
- If you want to stop second-guessing your own teaching methods,
- If you want to be the determining factor in the success of your students,

…then this book is for you!

Chapter 1

What is Differentiated Instruction, and Why Do We Differentiate?

We Sow before We Reap

If I can be successful on this step on which I stand
I might consider grasping onto your extended hand
For sometimes all I need is just a hand to help me rise
On ladders that reach onward into new uncharted skies.

I cannot climb the ladder without treading every rung
One leads to another, songs don't end until they're sung
Birds aren't free until they've flown
Moons rise before they sleep
Success is built upon success
We sow before we reap.

—Elizabeth Breaux

Differentiated Instruction is often referred to as part of the "new wave" in education, but Differentiated Instruction has been around for years. Differentiated Instruction is the practice of teaching each student in a manner that will accommodate how he/she learns best.

Many teachers are reluctant to differentiate, because the old theory of "one size fits all" was, for years, commonplace in our classrooms. A close, honest look, however, will reveal that no two students are the same. They come in a variety of sizes and shapes. We would never consider buying the same size shirt for all third graders and expect that all would fit. We understand that students have not all been exposed to the same types of environments. We would not assume that a student who has never ventured further than the edges of town would possess the same life experiences as one who vacationed overseas last summer.

Students learn differently. Some are more visual than auditory; most are kinesthetic in that they learn by doing (as we do in life in general); some need extended time to grasp concepts fully; some prefer a quiet, still atmosphere, while others are more open-minded when in motion. The list goes on and on. So why is it that we often rely on the same lesson plans and use the same methods of teaching for an entire class?

In the real world, we know better than that. Let's consider two sisters. One is two years of age and the other is four. They look strikingly similar; however, their personalities are extremely different. One is independent, outgoing, and has a long attention span. The other is shy, reluctant to meet strangers, and has a short attention span. Parenting must be differentiated in order to meet the needs of both.

Parents understand the need to differentiate parenting. We know instinctively that what fosters growth in one may actually inhibit growth in another. We have not been given any manuals or worksheets to assist us in parenting. Most of us have never attended seminars on "Differentiated Parenting." We just do what is best for each child because that is what makes the most sense. Yet we get into our classrooms and often lose our ability to think in practical, real-life, common sense terms.

Now let's contemplate the lives of a couple who have raised three children, all of whom are unique individuals with distinct, yet exceptional, characteristics. All have faced and overcome challenges with the help of two parents who fully understood the need to raise them all as separate entities and to differentiate their parenting to meet the children's individual needs. This was not an easy task but certainly a practical one. The following descriptions of each of the children are in the words of their mother, Denise Hebert. No one else could have given a more thorough, accurate, and heartfelt description of each child. Note that Denise is also a school teacher who has made it her mission to teach her students with regard to individual needs and differences. After reading the descriptions of her children, you'll understand why.

Jencie Marie

Jencie was diagnosed with Attention Deficit Disorder (ADD) in the fifth grade. She is really shy and has a hard time looking others in the eye. She is very kind-hearted and cries when she sees others hurt or upset. During her school years, we had to wake her at the same time every morning. She had to do things in the same order every morning (use the restroom, eat breakfast, brush teeth, dress, fix hair, come downstairs, put on shoes, etc.) If any part of her routine was interrupted, she was lost for the day. We had to allow her to "do her own thing." Her room was a total mess (you could not even see the floor), but she was organized in her own way. She could always find anything if asked, and she also knew where all of our things and her brother's and sister's things were. She always had her school work. She was never late for school or practices. She struggled when it came to academics, but she worked very hard. She prepared in advance for all events. The night before a game her bag was packed and checked three times. She would get up in the morning and check it three more times. She never forgot anything. I don't recall ever having to bring money, books, uniforms, etc., to school because she'd forgotten them. She was just super responsible. Today as always she is very creative and works well in small settings. She is currently working in the public school system in Lafayette, LA.

Andrew Joseph

Andrew is the middle child. He was diagnosed with Attention Deficit Hyperactivity Disorder (ADHD) when he was in high school. As a child he would climb anything that was at least eight feet tall and then jump! He would hide from us in stores. He would get lost, but he always found us. (We eventually stopped taking him to stores!) He was smart but did not have good habits, and we could never train him to do things in a systematic way. He was on the honor roll until he reached junior high school and then never again until his senior year when he finally realized what he had to do to make things work. He had to find out in his own way and time. Although it was difficult we knew we had to allow him to do that. Even today he is rarely on time, and he always forgets something. He usually ends up borrowing things, or he has to call Jencie to bring things to him at school. He is always out of lunch money and ends up having to borrow from someone. When he was younger, his nickname was "Contrare" (French for "contrary") because if we said "white" he said "black." When cleaning his room he would remove everything from the drawers and closets, thereby creating a bigger mess before he would begin neatly replacing all items, one at a time. He questioned/challenged all rules big and small. If he decided that it was worth the consequence, he broke the rule, knowing what was ahead. He was always bigger and stronger than the other children, yet he always sided with the underdog. He was basically extremely difficult, and we constantly had to try new things to use as punishments and rewards. On the other hand, he is very musically inclined. He plays the saxophone and taught himself to play the guitar. He has always been good at anything he decided to do. He was recently awarded a full football scholarship to the University of Louisiana.

Selina

Selina is dyslexic. She has brought life to this family. She lights up a room because she is so full of life and simply loves life. She is a hard worker. Give her a list and she'll get it done. She is the cleanest/neatest of the three children. She can get any job done in a short amount of time. She is very focused. She loves children and is very good with them. She works well with her hands. She can create new hair styles, dances, makeup, collages, etc. She would have been a hippy had she lived in the 60's. She's just a free bird. She packs on the morning of her events and runs around trying to get things all together, yet she rarely forgets anything. She will ask for things she needs on the day she needs them (money, supplies, gifts, etc.), but will leave early to get them and will not be late. She rarely plans anything in advance. She is not afraid to share her feelings about things. We do not need to guess with her. She is very verbal, and that sometimes gets her into trouble. She is not very good with boundaries, personal space, etc., and is repeatedly being told to "Back Up!" She has attracted people to her since she was an infant. This is wonderful to see and yet scary at the same time. She is currently a junior in high school.

"Life is never boring at home!" says Denise. "I probably needed anti-anxiety medications when I was younger, but I refused to give in and take them. So my husband Jay and the kids just call those my 'crazy days.' Jay has an attention deficit disorder, himself, so he often has no clue as to what is going on! Time and again we have to pull him back into the conversations. 'Hello…we are talking to you!' "

When we asked Denise how many books she's read on "Differentiated Parenting," she simply laughed at us. We think she and Jay should write the book!

Let's consider yet another real-life example of differentiation, the fast-paced American society, where many of us rely on the fast-food industry. One day we are hungry and are craving fried chicken… specifically some crispy wings with fries. We go into the restaurant and are told that only one dish is being provided today. It consists of two thighs, a slice of whole wheat bread, and salad. Because we are really hungry, we eat the food, even though it is not what we were craving. Would we go back to the same restaurant, or would we prefer to go to one where the order would be tailored to our particular, individual liking?

In life, we understand that we are all different. We recognize the fact that we all have different needs, different abilities, different likes and dislikes. We accommodate for those differences by seeking and affording ourselves variety and choice in all things that matter to us. We are in perpetual search of the perfect "fit." Without differentiation in choice, life would be a virile venture.

With that in mind, let's explore how Differentiated Instruction works in the classroom. If we are to effectively differentiate instruction, we must change how we teach the material, how we allow students to practice and obtain the new information, and how we permit them to express their knowledge of newly processed information. The only way to effectively create and implement this type of change is to know our students. (See Chapter 2 for more detailed information.)

Differentiated Instruction offers the learner a variety of techniques which create a change in the teaching and/or learning process in one or more of the following ways:

1. It provides students with diverse **methods** of acquiring knowledge.

2. It provides students with a variety of **strategies** to aid them in deepening their understanding of the acquired knowledge and provide them different ways of retaining new materials and ideas.

3. It provides students with an array of **assessments** ensuring that all students within one class setting can demonstrate their level of mastery of a skill regardless of their individual differences, abilities, and needs.

Take a close look at the following list of teaching *methods* and *strategies* and some of the authentic *assessments* that these methods and strategies might produce. Are you familiar with all of them? Do you use them regularly in your classroom? If so, how often? Do you want to know more about them?

Differentiated Instruction
Methods, Strategies, and Assessments

Method	Strategy	Assessment
brainstorming	interest groups	write a short story
varied text	Multiple Intelligences	design a game
Curriculum Compacting	interview	write a poem
	Connect Four	create a chart
Varied Questioning	Cooperative Grouping	draw a diagram
diagrams	debate	write a skit
peer tutoring	Tiered Assignments	make a commercial
Team Teaching	hands-on activities	complete a group project
Centers	study groups	debate a topic
technology	Anchoring Activites	critique a topic
guest speaker	silent reading	design a new product
hands-on modeling	RAFT	develop & illustrate a cartoon
discussions	venn diagrams	complete a demonstration
audio books	graphic organizers	develop a solution
interview	technology	write a news article
Jigsaw Puzzles	Progressive Pockets	

Depending on how they are implemented, some of the *methods* and *strategies* can be interchangeable. Let's look at the following examples.

Example 1:

Ms. Paul is a world history teacher who is beginning to teach a unit on the Gulf War. For the focus activity, she contacts a veteran soldier who agrees to be *interviewed* by the class. Ms. Paul has prepared questions that students will ask the soldier during the interview. *The **interview** is the **method** of instruction.*

As a follow-up activity, students complete a group project that involves the creation of a timeline of events that occurred during the Gulf War. They are required to use **technology** to research the information necessary to complete the timeline. *This **strategy** allows students to deepen their knowledge of the material by researching and organizing it in a timeline.*

Hence, the **interview** was used as a **method** for helping students acquire knowledge while **technology** was used as a **strategy** to deepen students' current knowledge and increase retention of the material.

Example 2:

Mr. Christie, another world history teacher, presents the same information. He develops a virtual field trip where the students explore the topic of the Gulf War. ***Technology*** is used here as a **method** of instruction.

Niki, an honor student, decides to **interview** her uncle who fought in the Gulf War. She is able to ask questions based on the information attained from the virtual field trip. This **interview** serves as a **strategy** used to deepen her knowledge of the previously studied material.

Hence, **technology** was used as a **method** for helping students acquire knowledge while the **interview** was used as a **strategy** to deepen students' current knowledge and increase retention of the material.

Just as "variety is the spice of life," differentiation is the spice of learning. Our students should enter our rooms every single day without a clue as to what types of methods and teaching strategies have been prepared for the lesson. Each new lesson should be another venture created with various likes, dislikes, abilities, levels of readiness, Learning Styles, Multiple Intelligences, etc., in mind. That is certainly not to say that we will not use some of the same teaching strategies, techniques, and methods on various occasions, but with the multitudes of choices out there, none should ever become redundant.

In Chapter 4 we will explore some of these methods and strategies and include practical, doable activities that are certain to spice up your classroom. But before that, let's prepare for the venture with Chapters 2 and 3.

Chapter 2
Know Your Students

Like any young teacher I thought that I knew
What it was that I still didn't know
I could have improved but the students removed
Any chances that I had to grow
After all my hard work, my plans still got shirked
By those vermin referred to as "students"
Practical planning and cautious examining
Still couldn't foster exuberance.
If only they'd done what I'd told them they should
In the manner in which I had planned
We could have foregone the disdain and the scorn
That occurred when I tried to demand.

In retrospect now I can see that the blunder
Was one that I hadn't perceived
While blaming the students' inadequate prudence
I was the one I deceived.
My methods were lacking appeal and attraction
No wonder that I couldn't see
Those blinders I wore while I lowered their scores
Were fooling nobody but me!

—Elizabeth Breaux

Each year we teachers are presented with 25 to 150 new students. To effectively teach them, we must become acquainted with how they learn best and what they enjoy most with regard to teaching methods. We cannot differentiate our instruction to meet the needs of each child until we discover how each learns best.

Think about the first time you met your best friend. It may have been at work, at a party, or at school. It may have been through a mutual friend, or maybe it was simply a chance meeting. It is not unusual to feel a spark or a connection with someone during a first meeting, a connection that grows deeper as you discover more about their life and personality.

After many years and countless conversations, this person became your best friend. You became familiar with their political views, morals, values, religious beliefs, and many other intimate details of their life. You slowly developed an intuition in regard to their likes and dislikes and how they might feel about particular topics and situations. You learned how to make them laugh and understood what made them cry. You learned when to lend a helping hand and when to listen in silence. With each interaction and conversation, you gained the knowledge that enabled you to become a better friend. That knowledge might include:

- childhood background
- educational history
- relationship with parents and siblings
- likes and dislikes
- values and morals
- religious beliefs
- interests and hobbies
- career choices
- motivations
- personality and style
- health or emotional issues
- favorite foods

It would be difficult to be a best friend to someone without first possessing an abundance of personal knowledge about them. Choosing a restaurant or a movie without knowing what types of foods or films they like would be challenging. Buying an appropriate birthday gift would be a "hit or miss" venture. We must get to know a person if we are to serve their needs, wants, and desires. The same premise holds true in education.

With the start of each new school year comes the fear of the unknown: "Who will be in my class this year?" Classroom rosters do not calm our fears, because they simply provide us with names. The apprehension comes from not knowing personalities, needs, Learning Styles, levels of readiness, etc. Just as it is important to know vital information so as to be a good friend, we must know vital information about our students if we are to successfully teach them. To facilitate success in each child, we must know how each is affected by various methods of instruction.

This seemingly formidable task, however, can be quite simple; the information gathered can make your classroom a more nurturing, motivating, successful environment where students can express themselves as individuals.

"Where do I begin?" you ask. In this chapter we will provide the information and the tools that will assist you in getting to know your students from the very first day of school:

- Interest Inventory
- Multiple Intelligences
- Learning Styles

Interest Inventory

On the first day of school, take the time to begin the process of getting to know your students. Start by giving them an interest inventory. This activity is a great ice-breaker and one that students typically enjoy because it is about them! It can be something as simple as the inventories on pages 12–13.

Don't forget to complete your own interest inventory and share it with your students. Allow them to ask questions and then model the appropriate ways to respond. Students want to know their teachers. Sharing information about yourself will initiate the vital establishment of trust.

Allow students to share their own interest inventories with the class, but only if they choose to do so. (Sometimes those who initially choose not to share will be more inclined to do so once they hear others sharing.) This activity facilitates the bonding of the group. If space is available in the classroom, you may want the students to post their inventories on the wall, but again only if they choose to do so.

Interest Inventory
Who Am I?

What is your full name? _____

List your family members: _____   _____
                          _____   _____
                          _____   _____

Do you have a pet? If so, what kind? _____

What is your favorite subject? _____

What do you most enjoy doing?_____
_____
_____

What are your favorite TV shows and movies? Can you explain why?
_____
_____

What type(s) of music do you like? _____
_____

What is your favorite color? _____

What is the last book you read?_____

Where did you go on your last vacation? _____

Where would you like to go on vacation?_____

What types of classroom activities do you like best? _____
_____
_____
_____

Tell about a special moment in your life. _____
_____
_____
_____
_____

Interest Inventory
Who Am I?

Choose the answer which best describes you by either circling the correct answer or filling in the blank.

My favorite subject is: Math   Reading/Language
                             Science   Social Studies

I have 1 2 3 4 5 6 brothers and/or sisters.

I am the   oldest middle youngest child in my family.

I have a pet. yes no

What type of pet do you have? _____

My favorite color is:
red black green orange purple yellow white

My favorite sport is: basketball football   baseball soccer hockey
                       dancing   volleyball running tennis golf

I like to do _____ in my free time.

My favorite game is _____.

I like being outdoors indoors.

My favorite TV show is _____.

I have do not have a computer at home.

I like/dislike swimming.

My favorite food is: pizza   hamburgers   hotdogs
                     chicken   meat and veggies _____ other

My favorite snack is: chips   ice cream   fruit
                     crackers   cookies   candy
                     popcorn   _____ other

Multiple Intelligences

Another way to get to know your students is to give them a Multiple Intelligences inventory. Before we look at an inventory, we must first understand the Theory of Multiple Intelligences and how it was derived.

In the 1900s, Alfred Binet, a psychologist, was charged with the task of finding a method of identifying whether or not a child would be successful in school. To the amazement of all, Binet developed the "intelligence test," his measure for the IQ—"intelligence quotient." He defined the IQ as a person's mental age (the age of intellectual development in an individual's thinking ability) divided by chronological age and multiplied by 100. The use of his intelligence test quickly spread and soon became the measure of "giftedness." A question remained, however: Could intelligence be accurately determined by basing it solely on this intelligence quotient?

Howard Gardner, a professor of cognition and education at the Harvard Graduate School of Education, studied cognitive science and neuroscience—the study of the mind and brain. He recognized that there were many different and discrete facets of cognition. He determined that people have different cognitive strengths and contrasting cognitive styles. This determination led him to believe that an IQ test, used in isolation, may not truly account for the natural gifts and abilities of artists like Pablo Picasso and composers like Beethoven. His question was this: Were these extremely gifted, talented, and accomplished people highly intelligent, or was there some other explanation?

Gardner determined that there were different types of intelligences. In his book *Multiple Intelligences—New Horizons*, he defines intelligence as "A bio-psychological potential of our species to process certain kinds of information in certain kinds of ways and that some intelligences were more prominent in individuals than others." He first concluded that there were seven intelligences and based his criteria for determining an intelligence on the following:

1. Could the intelligence be isolated in the brain?

2. Does the intelligence exist in prodigies, savants, and exceptional individuals?

3. Does the intelligence have an identifiable set of core operations (what you are capable of doing because of this intelligence)? Is it activated by internal or external information? (Example of core operations: Musical Intelligence is sensitive to pitch, tone, rhythm, and harmony.)

4. Was there an identifiable set of stages of growth starting at birth and developing throughout life?

5. Does the intelligence have evolutionary history—could it be traced throughout the homo sapiens evolution?

6. Does the intelligence support experimental psychology? (Can the intelligence identify specific tasks that can be observed and measured?)

7. Could the intelligence be measured by using psychometric tests? Could the tests identify, measure, and quantify human behavior related to the intelligence?

8. Was the intelligence symbolized by its own set of images or symbols? (Symbols are defined as "culturally contrived systems of meaning that capture and convey important forms of information.")

In 1983, Gardner developed his Theory of Multiple Intelligences which suggests that each individual is born with all 7 intelligences and has been encrypted with a personalized set of these intelligences. The strength of each intelligence varies from person to person, and all intelligences can be developed throughout a person's life.

Gardner's 7 Types of Intelligences

1. *Logical-Mathematical*: Children with this intelligence are often drawn to arithmetic problems, strategy games, and experiments. They are interested in patterns, categories, and relationships between things.

2. *Linguistic*: Children with this kind of intelligence often enjoy doing crossword puzzles, telling stories, reading, and writing.

3. *Musical:* Musical children are singers and/or incessant drummers. They usually have a heightened sense of sounds around them that others may miss. They are often astute listeners.

4. *Spatial*: These children view the world in images and pictures. They are often fascinated with things such as puzzles and mazes. They enjoy drawing and building things (with Legos, etc.), and are frequent daydreamers.

5. *Bodily-Kinesthetic:* These children are good athletes, dancers, woodworkers, craftsmen, etc., because they process knowledge through bodily sensations.

6. *Interpersonal*: Children with this intelligence are often leaders among their peers because they are good at communicating, and they are usually very perceptive when it comes to others' feelings and motives.

7. *Intrapersonal:* These children may be shy, but they are self-motivated. They are very aware of their own feelings.

Later, Gardner added *Naturalist Intelligence,* which he defines as "the ability to find patterns and relate to the natural world." He has considered adding a facet of Spiritual Intelligence, which he calls *Existential Intelligence.* In his book *Multiple Intelligences—New Horizons* he describes it as "the intelligence of big questions." He bases this intelligence on the fundamental principles of humans' ability to ponder thought-provoking questions such as:

- "Why do we live?"
- "Why do we die?"
- "What is going to happen to us?"
- "What is love?"

Although *Existential Intelligence* meets some of Gardner's criteria for intelligence, he is hesitant to give it the honor of the ninth intelligence. In his book *Multiple Intelligences—New Horizons,* Gardner states, "I shall continue for the time being to speak of 8½ intelligences."

His Theory of Multiple Intelligences, although initially written for psychologists, was quickly embraced by educators as a new way or means of differentiating for learners' needs (see figures 2.1–2.8, pp. 18–25). Understanding children's intelligences assists us in:

- providing the most appropriate activities for individual learners.
- providing students with authentic assessments.
- helping students build on their strengths and weaknesses.
- making students responsible for their own learning.
- motivating students.
- tailoring lessons to accommodate all learners.

Ask your students to complete a *Multiple Intelligences* inventory (see figures 2.9–2.12, pp. 26–30). Share the findings and discuss the different intelligences with them. This will give them a deeper appreciation of themselves and will encourage them to explore reasons for their likes, dislikes, behaviors, etc. Allow students to keep their profiles either on the wall or in a safe place where they can be easily referenced throughout the school year. Be sure to record all results on the *Know Your Students* sheet (see figure 2.15, p. 37) to be utilized as a quick reference.

Throughout the school year, recognize the students and their intelligences by incorporating activities from all intelligences.

Example: Mr. Mathieu teaches world history. He begins his lesson by asking students to list items that are operated through the use of electricity. After a discussion, he introduces his lesson about life before electricity. The students continue to study the way life has changed and the jobs that were created due to the invention of electricity. Mr. Mathieu decides to vary the students' assignments in accordance with their Multiple Intelligences, thereby modifying the final assessment of the lesson. His goal is for his students to understand the changes caused by electricity. He assigns the following activities:

> *Logical-Mathematical Intelligence*—Create a timeline showing the evolution of electricity over the years.
>
> *Linguistic Intelligence*—Write an essay discussing how life changed after the invention of electricity.
>
> *Musical Intelligence*—Write a song, jingle, or rap that depicts the changes in American life since the invention of electricity.
>
> *Spatial Intelligence*—Draw pictures of life before and after electricity. Compare and contrast the pictures.
>
> *Bodily-Kinesthetic Intelligence*—Build a model of a city and explain the problems that might occur when attempting to provide the city with electricity.
>
> *Interpersonal Intelligence*—Write a newspaper article about how American life changed the way people interacted after the invention of electricity.
>
> *Intrapersonal Intelligence*—Imagine that you are living during the years of the invention of electricity. Write a journal entry describing your feelings about the invention and how it changes your life.
>
> *Naturalistic Intelligence*—Write an essay describing how the invention of electricity will affect nature.

The old saying, "There is more than one way to skin a cat," applies most appropriately when we consider a classroom of students with varying intelligences. Remember that the objectives for the lesson are universal, but the strategies and assessments can be varied to address and meet each individual's needs in the manner that allows him/her to best meet the objectives. When instruction is personalized, it becomes more meaningful to the learner.

Figure 2.1
Logical-Mathematical Intelligence—"Number Smart"

Definition: Logical-Mathematical Intelligence is the ability to effectively use numbers and solve problems.

Characteristics:
1. Thinks abstractly and conceptually
2. Discerns logic and reason while carrying out mathematical operations or solving complex problems
3. Recognizes mathematical patterns, their relationships, and how they relate to all aspects of life
4. Loves numbers, mathematical formulas, and operations
5. Enjoys solving complex problems and analyzing circumstances, including peoples' behavior

Famous People:
Galileo
Nicolaus Copernicus
Pythagoras of Samos
Rene Descartes
Bill Gates
Chris Gardner
J. P. Morgan

Careers:
computer programmer
accountant
statistician
stockbroker
scientific researcher
data analyst
math teacher

Learns Best By:
inference
classifying
generalizations
using numbers

Classroom Behaviors Exhibited:
builds things
doodles with math problems
thinks deeply

Prefers Classes Involving:
charts
experiments
statistical data
diagrams
timelines
graphs
problem solving
logic games
sequencing

Figure 2.2
Linguistic Intelligence—"Word Smart"

Definition: Linguistic Intelligence is the ability to master language, both spoken and written, and to express personal viewpoints and the feelings of others.

Characteristics:
1. Communicates with ease, grace, and eloquence, a person's feelings, thoughts, or ideas
2. Understands the dynamics of the meanings of words and figures of speech and comprehends language to its fullest degree
3. Enjoys reading, writing, and speaking
4. Persuades others
5. Enjoys leading a meeting or making public speeches

Famous People:
William Shakespeare
Ernest Hemingway
J. K. Rowling
Steven King
Agatha Christie
Edgar Allen Poe

Learns Best By:
reading
writing
talking
hearing

Prefers Classes Involving:
writing activities
short stories
poems
debates
presentations
silent reading
crossword puzzles
storytelling
discussions
telling jokes

Careers:
author
poet
attorney
politician
debater
editor
writer

Classroom Behaviors Exhibited:
talking
passing notes
writing letters or stories
reading

Figure 2.3
Musical Intelligence—"Sound Smart"

Definition: Musical Intelligence is the ability to learn by recognizing tonal patterns, rhythms, and music in all facets of life.

Characteristics:
1. Hears pitch, melody, beats, and tones
2. Has a passion for music and sound to the degree of creating or emulating tones, melody, and beats in many forms
3. Enjoys studying or working with music in the background
4. Uses music to deepen personal relationships
5. Exhibits sensitivity to tones and sounds in nature

Famous People:
Wolfgang Mozart
Johann Sebastian Bach
Prince
Elvis Presley
Michael Jackson

Learns Best By:
hearing
rhythm
sounds

Prefers Classes Involving:
song writing
performances
technological animations with
  music
acting
chanting
producing a commercial
writing a play

Careers:
song writer
musician
singer
composer
film maker
sound engineer

Classroom Behaviors Exhibited:
tapping their feet or pencil
humming
singing

Figure 2.4
Spatial Intelligence—"Picture Smart"

Definition: Spatial Intelligence is the ability to learn by visualization.

Characteristics:
1. Thinks and reasons in images and pictures
2. Can abstractly visualize mind images and recreate or connect them to events or facts
3. Visualizes what one wants in life and obtains it
4. Is capable of using one's mind to represent the spatial world
5. Possesses highly developed memorization skills

Famous People:
Vincent van Gogh
Michelangelo Buonarroti
Claude Monet
Minoru Yamasaki
Amelia Earhart
Ansel Adams

Learns Best By:
pictures
images
models

Prefers Classes Involving:
drawing
venn diagrams
models
maps
dioramas
cartoons
brochures
flow charts
paintings
photography

Careers:
artist
architect
interior decorator
sculptor
cinematographer
photographer
engineer
surveyor

Classroom Behaviors Exhibited:
doodling
drawing pictures
stacking or building objects
daydreaming

Figure 2.5
Bodily-Kinesthetic Intelligence—"Body Smart"

Definition: Bodily-Kinesthetic Intelligence is the ability to use the body with grace or to produce and tell a story without the use of words.

Characteristics:
1. Learns by doing and/or moving the body
2. Possesses a keen sense of awareness of one's own body and knowing its limits
3. Possesses a greater awareness of body language and using it in communication
4. Controls the body and moves objects with precision
5. Mimics a task after seeing it performed

Famous People:
  Reggie Bush
  Heidi Klum
  Michael Jordan
  David Beckham
  Lebron James
  Gene Kelly
  Fred Astaire
  Rafael Nadal
  Anna Pavlova

Learns Best By:
  doing
  using the body
  hands-on activities
  moving around

Prefers Classes Involving:
  role play
  creating a dance or hand
    game
  games
  using manipulatives
  field trips
  charades

  demonstrations
  puppetry
  impersonations
  miming
  exercise

Careers:
  model
  athlete
  dancer
  exercise instructor
  choreographer
  gymnast
  mime

Classroom Behaviors Exhibited:
  walking around
  fidgeting
  stretching

Figure 2.6
Interpersonal Intelligence—"People Smart"

Definition: Interpersonal Intelligence is the ability to discern the intentions, perspectives, feelings, and motivations of others.

Characteristics:
1. Sympathizes and empathizes with others and shows a genuine understanding for others
2. Enjoys being around groups of people and friends
3. Gives advice freely and seeks advice from others regularly
4. Possesses leadership skills
5. Creates deeper, more meaningful relationships with others

Famous People:
Oprah Winfrey
Ghandi
Martin Luther King
Karl Marx
Dr. Ruth
Harry Truman
Dr. Joyce Brothers

Learns Best By:
understanding others' feelings
creating rules
building relationships with others
collaborating
receiving feedback

Prefers Classes Involving:
cooperative learning groups
peer teaching
team activities
conducting interviews
projects dealing with the
  community
point of view characterizations
presentations

Careers:
sociologist
politician
public relations personnel
salesperson
administrator
arbitrator

Classroom Behaviors Exhibited:
talking
passing notes
texting
being friends with everyone
wanting to work in groups
helping others

Figure 2.7
Intrapersonal Intelligence—"Self Smart"

Definition: Intrapersonal Intelligence is having a deep understanding of one-self (knowing who you are), the meaning of your life, the purpose of your life, and what you are capable of doing.

Characteristics:
1. Self-reflects and becomes one with feelings, thoughts, ideas, values, and beliefs
2. Is capable of being highly intuitive, strong willed, determined, self-confident, and motivated to achieve success
3. Possesses wisdom and insight and seeks to aid and assist others in need
4. Enjoys spending time alone meditating and reflecting about life
5. Is driven to learn more about oneself through seminars or counseling

Famous People:
Joan of Arc
George Patton
Joel Osteen
Anne Frank
Helen Keller
Aristotle
Sigmund Freud

Learns Best By:
reflecting
feedback
goal setting
independent practice

Prefers Classes Involving:
independent projects
journal writing
free-choice time
concentrating
higher-order thinking activities
reasoning

Careers:
pastor/priest
therapist
psychologist
counselor
social worker

Classroom Behaviors Exhibited:
wants to work alone
does not share well with others
disagrees with others
wants to express feelings about
   classroom activities
reflects or daydreams

Figure 2.8
Naturalist Intelligence—"Nature Smart"

Definition: Naturalist Intelligence is the ability to classify and recognize patterns in the natural world.

Characteristics:
1. Nurtures and respects all living things
2. Protects and conserves the environment
3. Recognizes and classify objects in the natural world
4. Understands the effects of nature and how it affects humans
5. Recognizes weather conditions and their effect on society

Famous People:
Charles Darwin
John James Audubon
Louis and Clark
Jacques Costeau

Learns Best By:
being outdoors
observing nature
collecting objects in nature
caring for insects or pets

Prefers Classes Involving:
field trips
nature hikes
using the microscope
classifying objects
organizing information
researching information
collecting specimens

Careers:
archaeologist
farmer
gardener
botanist
geologist
florist
environmental activist
meteorologist
veterinarian
forest ranger

Classroom Behaviors Exhibited:
stays too long outside
brings insects to class
collects objects in nature
will not harm any creature
gazes outside

Figure 2.9
Determine Your Multiple Intelligences

Circle the number next to each statement that best describes you. Total the number of circles in each part.

Part 1
1. I have pets and genuinely love animals.
2. I have a recycling system at home.
3. I enjoy being outside and doing outdoor activities.
4. I am interested in social issues and human motivation.
5. I can name different types of trees, leaves, flowers, and plants.
6. I understand global environmental issues.
7. I like to classify new information for easy learning.
8. I like gardening.

Total _____

Part 2
1. I know my strengths and weaknesses.
2. I like working alone rather than in a group.
3. I believe in giving my all when something is important to me.
4. I like reflecting about my life and what is important to me.
5. I have a deep belief in fairness and social justice.
6. I must have a good attitude to learn.
7. I need to know why a task is important before beginning it.
8. I have strong moral beliefs.

Total _____

Part 3
1. I can sing in key and understand pitch.
2. I know how to play musical instruments.
3. I like moving to the beat.
4. I enjoy listening to the sounds in nature.
5. I can remember lyrics of a song easily.
6. I often tap to a beat.
7. I enjoy listening to music when I am working.
8. I like making music.

Total _____

Part 4
1. I am structured.
2. I like working with numbers.
3. I enjoy brain teasers and other logic games.
4. I have a keen desire to make sense of things.
5. I find examples to support a general point of view.
6. I can mentally complete calculations more quickly than others.
7. I enjoy looking at data and statistically analyzing problems.

8. I am a problem solver.

Total _____

Part 5
1. I enjoy sports.
2. I am active in my lifestyle.
3. I learn best with "hands-on" activities.
4. I use hand gestures and other body language to express myself.
5. I enjoy working with tools or making things with my hands.
6. I like amusement park rides, even the most thrilling ones.
7. I enjoy dancing.
8. I problem-solve while walking or running.

Total _____

Part 6
1. I enjoy group work.
2. I am defined as a "social butterfly."
3. I believe friends are important.
4. I enjoy giving advice to others.
5. I like taking the lead and getting it done.
6. I am a "team player."
7. I prefer group study versus independent study.
8. I prefer chatting as opposed to having serious discussions.

Total _____

Part 7
1. I doodle often without knowing.
2. I enjoy reading material that has a lot of illustrations.
3. I can read a map without a problem.
4. I enjoy taking things apart and putting them back together.
5. I recall things more easily by formulating mental images.
6. I can learn better with diagrams, charts, and visuals.
7. I enjoy redecorating or rearranging a room.
8. I appreciate the arts.

Total _____

Part 8
1. I enjoy reading.
2. I like doing crossword puzzles and word games.
3. I say what I think in a debate or verbal argument.
4. I like lectures and speeches.
5. I can easily express myself in speech or writing.
6. I like to talk through problems.
7. I frequently use words some people may not know.
8. I prefer English and/or history classes.

Total _____

Fig. 2.10
Multiple Intelligences Profile

Directions: Color or shade in the totals from each part of the *Determine Your Multiple Intelligences* inventory. The results will help you to identify your personalized set of Multiple Intelligences. Remember that we are born with all of the intelligences and have the ability to enhance each with work and effort.

Multiple Intelligences Profile

Name_____

8	8	8	8	8	8	8	8
7	7	7	7	7	7	7	7
6	6	6	6	6	6	6	6
5	5	5	5	5	5	5	5
4	4	4	4	4	4	4	4
3	3	3	3	3	3	3	3
2	2	2	2	2	2	2	2
1	1	1	1	1	1	1	1
Part 1 Naturalist Intelligence	**Part 2** Intrapersonal Intelligence	**Part 3** Musical Intelligence	**Part 4** Logical-Mathematical Intelligence	**Part 5** Bodily-Kinesthetic Intelligence	**Part 6** Interpersonal Intelligence	**Part 7** Spatial Intelligence	**Part 8** Linguistic Intelligence

Fig. 2.11
Determine Your Multiple Intelligences

Circle each statement that describes you the best. Total the number of circles in each part.

Part 1 Naturalistic Intelligence
I like all animals and insects.
I know the names of different plants and flowers.
I like collecting rocks.
I recycle every day at home.
Total _____

Part 2 Intrapersonal Intelligence
I like being alone.
I get upset when someone is treated unfairly.
I get nervous around a lot of people.
I want to know why when given an assignment.
Total_____

Part 3 Musical Intelligence
I can play a musical instrument.
I often tap to the beat without hearing music.
I like singing.
I remember the words to different songs.
Total _____

Part 4 Logical-Mathematical Intelligence
I like math.
I like to sort objects by color, size, or shape.
I like to figure out how to do something on my own.
I like puzzles.
Total _____

Part 5 Bodily-Kinesthetic Intelligence
I like to play outdoors.
I like sports.
I like to dance.
I like to build things.
Total _____

Part 6 Interpersonal Intelligence
I like to be the leader.
I like working in a group.
I have a lot of friends.
I like to cheer up others who are sad.
Total _____

Part 7 Spatial Intelligence
I like to draw.
I like looking at pictures.
I doodle while doing other things.
I can remember an object/person's face after I see it one time.
Total _____

Part 8 Linguistic Intelligence
I like reading.
I like writing/telling a story.
I sound out words that I do not know.
I like to teach others how to do a task.
Total _____

Fig. 2.12
Multiple Intelligences Profile

Directions: Color in the totals from each part of the *Determine Your Multiple Intelligences* inventory. The results will help you identify your personalized set of Multiple Intelligences.

Multiple Intelligences Profile

Name_____

4	4	4	4	4	4	4	4
3	3	3	3	3	3	3	3
2	2	2	2	2	2	2	2
1	1	1	1	1	1	1	1
Part 1 Naturalist Intelligence	**Part 2** Intrapersonal Intelligence	**Part 3** Musical Intelligence	**Part 4** Logical-Mathematical Intelligence	**Part 5** Bodily-Kinesthetic Intelligence	**Part 6** Interpersonal Intelligence	**Part 7** Spatial Intelligence	**Part 8** Linguistic Intelligence

Learning Styles

A third way to get to know your students is to determine their Learning Styles. A learning style is the way a person acquires and processes new information. Each individual has five senses that are developed to different degrees. We use these senses daily to accomplish simple tasks, to learn new information, and to process information. Some people can listen and remember the information verbatim while others need to see a picture or the printed words. Others need to touch things in order to truly "see" them. Individuals possess all three of the following Learning Styles but use them at different stages and to different degrees in the learning process.

A Visual Learner:
1. learns by seeing and writing.
2. must think before understanding a topic.
3. needs silence while studying or processing information.
4. understands charts and graphs.
5. outlines information for faster processing or uses flashcards.
6. enjoys learning with animations.

An Auditory Learner:
1. learns by hearing.
2. comprehends information when read aloud.
3. enjoys explaining information.
4. loves music and beats.
5. learns through lectures and will often record them for future use.
6. enjoys studying with peers to discuss information.

A Tactile/Kinesthetic Learner:
1. learns by doing.
2. enjoys moving the body or manipulating objects.
3. likes to attend field trips.
4. loves games and sports.
5. enjoys using the computer.
6. uses flashcards to aid in learning.

In education, the evolutionary process of learning begins with the use of manipulatives. In elementary classrooms, especially kindergarten and first grade, students are taught how to add and subtract with the use of manipulatives. Most lessons require that students touch and feel so as to fully absorb meaning. This tactile/kinesthetic learning approach enables a child to think concretely about the subject matter before advancing toward more abstract problems.

As children mature, teachers begin to move away from the hands-on types of activities but do (typically) continue to use visual aids.

As students progress toward high school and college, lectures begin to replace visual aids and hands-on activities, and unfortunately those often become obsolete. Teachers begin to rely more on lecture because it allows them to cover a vast amount of information in a short amount of time. Expediting the curriculum, however, leads to a concern: *Are the students really processing the information so that learning occurs?* If students are not engaged in the learning process, they are probably not learning the material.

Incorporating activities that address the three Learning Styles will result in a deeper understanding of the topic, less time spent on review, increased retention of material, higher test grades, and higher academic success. All teachers can incorporate lessons that address the three Learning Styles, regardless of topic or subject matter, as can be seen in the following examples:

> Mrs. Noel is a teacher of a fourth-grade, self-contained class. She is responsible for teaching all of the core academic subjects—language arts, math, social studies, and science. She begins her unit on the solar system by requiring each student to name the planets in their proper order. She makes certain that her lesson's activities accommodate for the various Learning Styles of her students:
>
> - **Visual Learners:** Mrs. Noel creates a dynamic, animated presentation using video technology that details the eight planets. The presentation is loaded with great visual effects that highlight the important points. The visual representations reinforce the order of the planets. In addition, Mrs. Noel designs a vibrant bulletin board for additional reinforcement of the order of the planets.
>
> - **Auditory Learners:** Mrs. Noel gives the students a thorough explanation of the eight planets along with an easy mnemonic device that can be used any time for quick recall. She explains that the first letter in each word of the mnemonic device, **My Very Eager Mother Just Served Us N**oodles, represents the first letter in each of the planets: Mercury, Venus, Earth, Mars, Jupiter, Saturn, Uranus, and Neptune.
>
> - **Tactile/Kinesthetic Learner:** Mrs. Noel gives her students a picture of each planet. Each picture forms a three-dimensional shape that students will color, cut, and paste to create a mobile. This activity allows the students to manipulate each planet while piecing them together in their proper locations in the solar system.

It is easy to dismiss a lesson topic or skill as being one that does not lend itself well to differentiation in Learning Styles, but before buying in to that theory, consider that a body motion, dance, or any tapping/clapping game can be easily incorporated into any lesson regardless of the subject matter. Age, grade, and subject content are of little importance, as is exemplified below.

Peter, an eighth-grade tactile/kinesthetic learner, is struggling to remember the order of operations in math using a typical mnemonic device, **PEMDAS** *or Please Excuse My Dear Aunt Sally*. His math teacher, Mrs. Adams, decides that Peter might be able to remember the order if a hand movement (for this tactile/kinesthetic learner) was incorporated. She devises a kinesthetic mnemonic device that involves the following body parts, to which she points as she recites each: *1. Pupils, 2. Ears, 3. Muscles or Deltoids, and 4. Abdomen or Stomach.* They practice until Peter can point to each part of the body with ease. Then Mrs. Adams replaces the words with *1. Parenthesis, 2. Exponents, 3. Multiplication or Division, and 4. Addition or Subtraction.* Through the use of this kinesthetic mnemonic device, Peter is then able to remember the order of mathematical operations.

Fig. 2.13
Learning Styles Inventory

Check the most appropriate box next to each statement to determine your learning style.

Part 1

		Often		Sometimes		Seldom
1.	I prefer to read materials in a textbook than to listen to lectures.	☐	Often	☐	Sometimes	☐ Seldom
2.	I remember information when I put it on flashcards.	☐	Often	☐	Sometimes	☐ Seldom
3.	I enjoy doing word puzzles and crossword puzzles.	☐	Often	☐	Sometimes	☐ Seldom
4.	I prefer writing things down or taking notes when studying.	☐	Often	☐	Sometimes	☐ Seldom
5.	I can easily follow directions using a map.	☐	Often	☐	Sometimes	☐ Seldom
6.	I prefer to obtain new information by reading.	☐	Often	☐	Sometimes	☐ Seldom
7.	I like to picture something in my head when trying to remember it.	☐	Often	☐	Sometimes	☐ Seldom
8.	I enjoy making graphs and charts.	☐	Often	☐	Sometimes	☐ Seldom

Part 2

9.	I often read aloud to understand information.	☐	Often	☐	Sometimes	☐ Seldom
10.	I need someone to explain graphs and/or charts to me.	☐	Often	☐	Sometimes	☐ Seldom
11.	I prefer listening to the news on the radio as opposed to reading it in the newspaper.	☐	Often	☐	Sometimes	☐ Seldom
12.	I can learn how to spell a word better by repeating the spelling versus writing it down.	☐	Often	☐	Sometimes	☐ Seldom
13.	I prefer oral directions to written directions.	☐	Often	☐	Sometimes	☐ Seldom
14.	I prefer to listen to a book on tape than read it.	☐	Often	☐	Sometimes	☐ Seldom
15.	I remember phone numbers by repeating the number several times.	☐	Often	☐	Sometimes	☐ Seldom
16.	I prefer academic classes that give information via lecture.	☐	Often	☐	Sometimes	☐ Seldom

Part 3			
17. I enjoy doing hands-on activities.	☐ Often	☐ Sometimes	☐ Seldom
18. I play with the coins in my pocket or the keys in my hands.	☐ Often	☐ Sometimes	☐ Seldom
19. I learn best by doing.	☐ Often	☐ Sometimes	☐ Seldom
20. I learn better with physical activity.	☐ Often	☐ Sometimes	☐ Seldom
21. I find myself chewing gum or snacking while studying.	☐ Often	☐ Sometimes	☐ Seldom
22. I am very comfortable with hugging or touching others.	☐ Often	☐ Sometimes	☐ Seldom
23. I remember things best by writing them down multiple times.	☐ Often	☐ Sometimes	☐ Seldom
24. I learn more from a lab class setting versus a lecture.	☐ Often	☐ Sometimes	☐ Seldom

Scoring Directions: The following points apply to each.

Often = 5 points
Sometimes = 3 points
Seldom = 1 point

Look at your response to each question. For each separate part add up the number of points for Often (5 points each), Sometimes (3 points each), and Seldom (1 point each). Write them on the lines below. The part with the greatest number of points is your preferred learning style.

Part 1 — Visual Learner _____
Part 2 — Auditory Learner _____
Part 3 — Tactile/Kinesthetic Learner _____

Fig. 2.14
Learning Styles Inventory

Circle each statement that describes you the best. Total the number of circles in each part to determine your learning style.

Part 1 Visual Learner

I enjoy doing puzzles.

I prefer books with lots of pictures.

I like bright colors or objects.

I like to color or paint.

I remember people's faces more easily than I remember their names.

Total _____

Part 2 Auditory Learner

I like to talk.

I remember the words to songs.

I prefer listening to a book rather than reading it.

I learn by repeating information aloud.

I can easily follow verbal directions.

Total _____

Part 3 Tactile/Kinesthetic Learner

I fidget or move a lot.

I like building and creating new things.

I am comfortable touching others.

I enjoy sports or dancing.

I enjoy touching and feeling objects or books.

Total _____

Fig. 2.15
Know Your Students

Use this chart to compile students' information for easy access.

Name	Interest	Multiple Intelligence 1st (strongest)	Multiple Intelligence 2nd	Multiple Intelligence 8th (weakest)	Preferred Learning Style
(sample) Monticule, Monica	Movies	Intrapersonal	Logical Mathematical	Interpersonal	Visual

Chapter 3

Management for Differentiated Instruction
Two Critical Steps

Organization and Classroom Management

A well-organized and well-managed classroom is an ideal setting for learning. An ill-organized and ill-managed classroom is the foundation upon which thoughtful plans and good intentions die slow, laborious deaths. Without excellent classroom management, we cannot be excellent teachers. Even when the management is slightly flawed, we cannot effectively differentiate our instruction.

Have you ever wondered why "Differentiated Instruction" is considered an unthinkable concept to many teachers? Why the mere thought of teaching with individual differences in mind is shunned by even some of the most experienced and potentially great teachers? Wonder no more. Simply go into a classroom where a teacher is attempting to differentiate instruction in the absence of good management planning, and the utter chaos alone will answer your question. Without the groundwork, differentiation cannot be successful.

Organization and classroom management are categorically necessary foundation for the structure to survive. Without it, differentiation is impossible or at best ineffective. Any attempt to differentiate beforehand would be futile, leading to the very stress and exhaustion that often forces us to give up and return to the "tried and true" methods where all students are expected to be on the same page, at the same time, on the same day, with identical results. Impossible.

Ponder this question: Can a disorganized teacher also be an effective teacher? We've all known one who was. The fact, however, is that if that same teacher became better organized, he/she would be even more effective. Let's step into the classroom of a teacher whose organizational and managerial skills are lacking, yet he still manages to teach:

Mr. Scattered is one of the well-respected teachers at Central High. He has been teaching there for 29 years and is known for his ability to reach and educate even some of the toughest students. He is a master of history and has a natural ability for motivating and engaging students. Mr. Scattered is also a slob! However, in spite of the downright disarray of his classroom, teaching and learning survive. In spite of the fact that precious time is lost due to disorganization, his reputation as one of the "favorites" endures. On any given day, however, as much as 25% of instructional time is lost due to the disorganization. It looks something like this:

- Class begins late because Mr. Scattered is late.
- Students are tardy because punctuality is not a requirement in his classroom.

- Mr. Scattered begins his lesson before realizing that he cannot find some of the materials that he has prepared for today. He sends a student to the office to ask for copies. Precious teaching time is lost.
- Mr. Scattered returns test papers from the previous day. There is no set procedure for doing so, therefore a few more lost minutes are added to the day's total.

This is a typical day in Mr. Scattered's classroom. Yet despite all of this, he still manages to teach! He obviously has the people skills that have allowed him to build great relationships with his students, and he also possesses an immense knowledge of the subject matter. Unfortunately, he is lacking the managerial and organizational skills that would allow him more teaching time and make him a more effective teacher. Twenty-five percent more teaching time per day equates to 25% more teaching days per year!

The painful truth is that in order to differentiate instruction, we must plan well. Procedures must be in place and strictly enforced. Students should not be expected to be mind readers. We must teach them, with precision, the procedures that we expect them to follow and then enforce these procedures with absolute consistency. If we cannot do that, we cannot have effective differentiation of instruction.

Step into a well-organized and well-managed classroom where Differentiated Instruction is the norm, and you may not even notice all of the hard work that has gone into the impeccably flowing lesson. You may merely notice a stress-free teacher, engaged and motivated students, and a learning environment filled with structured noise, movement, and numerous learning possibilities. This is the teacher who seems to get all of the best students every year. This is the ground on which learning is fostered. This is the ground upon which learning is fun. This is the ground upon which teaching is most rewarding.

In her book, *Classroom Management—SIMPLIFIED*, Elizabeth Breaux teaches how to implement common classroom and school-wide procedures in a manner that enables the teacher to run the classroom efficiently and effectively and to make optimal use of teaching time. She states that:

One of the worst mistakes we make as teachers is assuming that the students already know our procedures. If we make this incorrect assumption, we are most certainly laying the groundwork for failure. Instead, place your students at ease from day one. Tell them that there are many procedures that they will be expected to follow and that you will teach them each procedure, one at a time, practicing each one with them. Also, take the fear of failure away from them by letting them know that you do not expect that they will implement the procedures properly in the initial stages but that you will simply remind them when they "mess up" so that the correct implementation of the procedure can become routine."

Breaux explains that in order to get students to follow our procedures, we must go through the three critical steps:

- **Teach** the procedure.
- **Practice** the procedure.
- **Implement** the procedure.

"So where do we start?" you ask. First, ponder the following questions when deciding upon the appropriate procedures for a given activity:

- How will physical movement take place in the classroom? Will there be directives in the form of verbal cues or auditory signals?
- Will students be placed into groups? If so, what are the specific procedures necessary to make group work effective and non-chaotic?
- Will supplies be readily available for use? Are there specific procedures for using supplies?
- How are the students to gain the attention of the teacher when help is needed?
- How will initial directives be given in a manner that ensures student understanding?

Once you are able to answer these questions, decide how you will present the new procedures to your class using the *Teach, Practice,* and *Implement* method.

Example:

Let's assume that you are planning an activity that requires students be placed into groups. You have already determined the groups based on Learning Styles and assigned students to each using colors to denote group assignments. The color of each child's group is written next to his/her name in your roll book. You are ready to begin the activity, but must first teach students the procedures that will be used. You decide that you will teach procedures for the following:

1. Getting into Groups
2. Acquiring the Teacher's Attention
3. Using Materials and Supplies

4. Talking

5. Assessment

How to Teach It

NOTE: Following are suggestions only.

1. **Getting into Groups**: Have desks prearranged in groups of four with a colored flag at each grouping: red, blue, green, yellow, or orange. As students enter the classroom, give them a colored assignment sheet and direct them to go to the designated group. (The color of the sheet denotes the group to which the students have been assigned.) When the tardy bell rings, explain to them that this will be the procedure that will be used from now on for "getting into groups." Go over the process that just took place. Tell them that from now on this process should run much more smoothly, so your expectation is that all group members will have been seated by the time the tardy bell rings.

2. **Acquiring the Teacher's Attention**: Tell students that their group's flag can now be taken down. In the event that the group needs the teacher's attention, the flag should be held up until the teacher responds. Once the question has been answered, it should be put down. Designate one child per group as the "flag holder." (Model "holding" as opposed to "waving" the flag!)

3. **Using Materials and Supplies**: Tell students that all supplies will be distributed to the groups. There should be no reason to move away from desks during the activity. If a situation arises, students should raise the flag and wait for the teacher to respond.

   NOTE: If you would prefer that your students acquire the supplies on an "as-needed" basis, designate one person as the "supplies manager."

4. **Talking**: Tell students that quiet talking amongst group members is allowed. Talking to the teacher is allowed, but the procedure for getting the teacher's attention (holding up the flag) must be followed. Talking to members of other groups is not allowed.

5. **Assessment**: Distribute the assessment rubric to each group. Give one to each child for this initial explanation, even though this particular activity might require that each group be graded using only one group rubric. Go through each item on the rubric, making certain

that students understand the procedure for earning and losing points throughout the implementation of the activity.

NOTE: You should note all requirements and possible points for each level of proficiency. Behavioral items should be included on the rubric so that students will understand that points can be earned or lost in regard to how well procedures are followed. This is an excellent way to keep students on task and activities flowing smoothly.

How to Practice It

NOTE: Allow students to practice all of the procedures. Encourage them to make mistakes so that everyone can see how "not" to do it. Praise them for all correct implementations, thank those who made the mistakes, and then redirect all to the proper implementations.

1. **Getting Into Groups**: Have students exit the room and practice the procedure for coming in and going directly to their groups. Time them. Remind them that all members must be seated before the tardy bell rings so that the group can be awarded the points on the rubric.

2. **Acquiring the Teacher's Attention**: Designate one group member from each group as the "flag holder" and encourage groups to ask questions. Practice going from one group to the next so that students can see this in action.

3. **Using Materials and Supplies**: Distribute the supplies. Tell students to discuss with group members whether or not additional supplies might be needed. If it is determined that additional supplies are needed, the flag holder must raise the flag and wait for the teacher.

4. **Talking**: Tell students within each group to talk to one another. Give them a minute or so to talk. If students are caught talking to anyone outside of the group the teacher must acknowledge and correct that mistake immediately.

5. **Assessment**: Give one assessment rubric to each group. Direct the group's attention to the behavioral items. Go over each one again. Have one group model incorrect implementation of the procedures and then discuss the repercussions, regarding points lost on the rubric, with the class.

How to Implement It

NOTE: We suggest that the teacher conduct the Teaching and Practicing sessions *on the day before the assignment will begin*. That way the implementation can begin at the beginning of class on the next day.

As students enter the room on the day after the Teaching and Practicing phases, begin implementation. Remember to remain utterly consistent. Correct any incorrect implementation immediately. Deduct points as necessary. Make certain that the students know that there is no room for error or negotiation. Make that point, and the procedures will work precisely as planned.

Planning for Differentiated Instruction

Differentiating instruction can be amazingly stress-free or exceptionally stressful. Chances are that in a random survey of teachers, many would describe it under one of those two categories. Further inquiry would likely reveal that the former category (stress-free) consists of teachers who are well-planned, and the latter category (stressful) of those who are not. Without proper planning, differentiation can be disastrous.

To many of us teachers, it may seem a bit odd to regard the planning phase as being Step 2 in the process, since we have always viewed planning as being the first step in all things that relate to teaching. In the case of differentiating, we must establish good classroom management through impeccable organization before we can even begin to plan a differentiated lesson. Then, in regard to planning, a proper differentiated lesson cannot be properly implemented if it is not well planned.

Ask any successful differentiator and he or she will tell you the more work that is put into the planning phase, the more successful and less stressful the lesson. The two go hand in hand. Another perk of good planning is that once a great lesson is planned, it can be used many times; the really hard work happens only once.

It is necessary to make several considerations in the preliminary stages of lesson creation. They include, but are certainly not limited to, the following:

1. Which standards, benchmarks, etc., are going to be addressed in the lesson?

2. What is the timeline of the lesson?

3. What are the specific goals and objectives of the lesson?

4. Which specific strategies and activities might work best for a particular group of students? (Have individual student abilities, likes/dis-

likes, needs, and Learning Styles been considered when making this determination?)

5. What has and has not worked in past lessons with these students?

Once these have been determined, the physical design of the lesson (with all of its components) can commence:

1. How will the teacher capture the attention of the students?
   - storytelling
   - connection with prior lesson
   - unexpected room design
   - surprising icebreaker
   - differentiated activity
   - other activity

2. How will the teacher take the class from a whole-group lesson introduction, through a smooth transition, and into a differentiated activity?

3. Is there a plan for teaching the procedures that will be used during the implementation of the activity?
   - movement around the room
   - talking to others
   - on-task behaviors
   - distribution and pick-up of materials and supplies
   - getting the teacher's attention

4. Is there a plan for room design?

5. Is the room clutter free and well-organized to allow for freedom of movement and smooth transitions?

6. Have all lesson materials been created, laminated (if appropriate), and arranged for usage?

7. Do all components of the activity include clear and concise directions, rubrics, score sheets, etc?

8. When and how will feedback be given?

When we consider all of the components that are necessary to prepare an effective differentiated lesson, it becomes apparent that it is hard work! This hard work, however, produces enormous returns:
   - The implementation is basically stress-free.
   - Behaviors that warrant disciplinary action are virtually eliminated.

- The teacher is afforded the time to give individual attention as needed.
- Students stay on task because they are engaged in the lesson.
- Student achievement rises.
- Self-esteem is fostered.
- Successes encourage future successes.

Let's venture into classrooms where Differentiated Instruction is being implemented through a variety of methods, strategies, and assessments. We hope that you will find most or all of them useful and beneficial. We have made every effort to provide you with activities that can be tailored to fit any grade level and subject area. Read on!

Chapter 4
Twelve Ways to
Differentiate

The Sum of My Parts

If the sum of my parts is what makes me my whole
And your parts are different from mine (I've been told)
Then your parts assembled should not look like mine
And mine should, of course, confirm separate designs

Designs that are different, too often in practice
Regarded as one using similar tactics
Expecting one whole to react as the other
When one is his own and the second another

If this sounds confusing then you should be me
Struggling and striving and yearning to see
The world through the parts that belong to the sum
A whole that's not I and I cannot become!

—Elizabeth Breaux
from *How the BEST TEACHERS Avoid*
the 20 Most Common Teaching Mistakes

1
Cooperative Grouping

Just before the game the coach surprised us with the news
He said the plans we'd made were not the ones that we would use
He gave us new positions, ones we'd never played before
And in spite of all the changes still expected us to score.

The quarterback would kick the ball, the center was to run
The big offensive linemen were to try to catch someone
The water boy would call the plays, the coach would run the clock
The trainer, though a little one, would tow the line and block.

There's outrage in the grandstand now, dissention on the field
The referee says "play the game," the kick-off seals the deal
There's mayhem on the sidelines, confusion in the huddle
And accusations flying that are anything but subtle…

—Elizabeth Breaux

What Is It?

Great coaches are great teachers. They recognize the strengths and weaknesses in individual players and plan with those differences in mind. They realize that the whole is the sum of its individual parts. Hence, they identify and develop individual strengths so that when all work simultaneously, the whole can be successful. Each member of the team must be successful if the team is to succeed. Because of that, coaches strive to use each player in the part that best suits the player and the team.

Team sports are truly cooperative endeavors. Once players begin to recognize each member as integral to the whole, they begin to affirm and trust one another. They learn to compromise, negotiate, and use criticism constructively. Along the way, they develop conflict-resolution skills.

Inside the classroom, Cooperative Grouping is an instructional strategy designed to maximize each student's ability while allowing students to work together to accomplish a shared goal. Cooperative Grouping activities occur AFTER direct instruction. Once the teacher has completed the instructional phase, students are placed into groups and given cooperative assignments that will allow them to practice what they have been taught.

NOTE: It is critical that students have a solid grasp of the material before they are placed into cooperative groups.

Group size should be limited to no more than 4–5 students per group. Makeup of groups should vary depending on the lesson. The makeup of groups should be continuously changing to meet the growing and changing abilities and needs of individual students, just as a coach's game plan is always subject to change. Group makeup could include students of mixed abilities, or it might be based upon one or more of the following:

- similar abilities
- readiness levels
- interests
- Multiple Intelligences
- Learning Styles

The ultimate success of Cooperative Grouping rests on the ability of the teacher to plan effectively. Proper planning for the implementation of Cooperative Grouping will remove the likelihood of one person carrying the load for the group. The teacher must provide individual group members with separate structured activities/roles/responsibilities that will ultimately enhance the final group product. This will ensure time on task and deepen knowledge levels. The activities must be precisely defined and described to the students. A teacher might select the roles for each person in a group, or in the case of the older, more mature students, might allow them to select their own roles in their cooperative group.

Each role must be vital to the success of the group, just as each player's position is vital to the success of the team. Each student must recognize the value in his/her role, or he/she will not perform. If each member is given an individual role that is graded according to its own set of criteria (rubric), the responsibility for the whole is felt by each individual member. All rely on one another for contributions to the whole.

Students must know the reason for the activity, its benefits, and the specific knowledge that should be acquired and demonstrated at the end of the activity. In short, if students know the benefit and purpose of the activity, it will be meaningful for them.

If each child's role is geared toward his/her individual needs, strengths, Learning Styles, etc., it can be the perfect Differentiated Instruction strategy. When planning a Cooperative Grouping activity, the teacher can either assign the predetermined roles or allow students to assign the roles once the group receives them. Following is an example of the makeup of a cooperative group:

1. leader

2. artist

3. researcher

4. presenter

5. writer

Because the students are forced to work as a team, cooperation and teamwork are vital. The writer cannot proceed without the work of the researcher. The artist cannot illustrate a piece of writing that is incomplete. The presenter cannot make an accurate presentation if he/she has not worked closely with the group throughout the process. All need a manager or leader to help make the process run efficiently.

Cooperative Grouping lends itself perfectly to addressing individual needs through differentiation of instruction. When properly planned and implemented, the rewards are numerous.

1. Students' socialization skills are developed.

2. Students' self-esteem is fostered as a result of their successes.

3. Students' knowledge and understanding of the topic is deepened.

4. Students' presentation and oral communication skills are enhanced.

5. Students' academic test scores improve.

Classroom Scenario

Southside Middle School is a low-performing school. Many students are complacent, unmotivated, and do not value education. Some have been retained throughout the years. As a result, in many classrooms there are over-aged students, some of whom are embarrassed by their age and size. Self-esteem is low due to the ongoing lack of successful experiences.

Mrs. Thomas is a veteran teacher whose passion for math is contagious. She is excited about the start of another school year. She is aware of the many challenges that she faces, but as usual she is ready and willing to face them.

Mrs. Thomas has learned that in order to make learning meaningful and engaging, she must incorporate many hands-on, real-life activities into all of her lessons. After several weeks of engaging her students in various dynamic lessons, she decides to create cooperative groups for the culminating project.

The Differentiated Way

Planning

1. Mrs. Thomas contemplates the upcoming unit in which she will teach students to calculate area using the appropriate mathematical formulas.

2. She plans the whole group/direct instruction portion of the lesson.

3. She ponders the real-life application of the mathematical formulas while creating a Cooperative Grouping activity that could be utilized in a real-life situation.

4. She determines the various tasks that would be necessary to ensure the success of the project.

5. She creates 6 groups of 4 students each (group makeup is based on ability, personality, and Multiple Intelligences) and designates each child's tasks (see figure 4.2, p. 58).

6. She obtains assignment folders for the groups. Each group will receive four colored folders (blue, green, yellow, red), one for each member. The colors provide distinction among the various roles.

7. She creates separate assignments with accompanying rubrics and places those in their coordinating folders.

8. She creates a rubric for the assessment of the final project.

9. She constructs a list of established rules and procedures that will guide the activity.

Implementation

As students enter the room, Mrs. Thomas gives each person a number (1–6) and instructs them to report to the corresponding group area. Desks are already arranged to form 6 groups of 4 members each. Colored folders have already been placed on the desks. The bell rings.

Mrs. Thomas begins by conducting a brief review of the various mathematical formulas for finding area, perimeter, etc. She conducts a short question/answer session to ascertain whether or not all students are ready to begin the Cooperative Grouping assignment.

She calls out names of each student in each group so as to designate folder colors.

Example: Group #1

1. Madison: Blue
2. Paul: Green
3. Simone: Yellow
4. Bailey: Red

Once students have attained the proper folders, Mrs. Thomas begins the explanation of the assignment, the rules and procedures, and the use of the rubrics. She instructs each student to open his/her folder and to read the individual instructions. She invites the students to ask procedural questions before the activity commences.

Students notice that each folder contains an explanation of the overall group assignment:

Group Assignment:

You are contractors who are bidding on a job for the school district. The job entails building an additional classroom for your school. The classroom addition should have the same dimensions as your current classroom. You know that several contractors (other groups) will be placing bids and that the contractor with the lowest bid will be awarded the job. You really want the job, but you don't want your bid to be too low, because you need to make a profit.

To submit a fair bid, you will need to determine the following:

1. dimensions of the room

2. dimensions of additional structures within the room

3. dimensions of windows and doors

4. materials needed and amounts of each

5. cost of materials

6. cost for delivery of materials

7. cost for labor

Once all of the above have been determined, you should be ready to place a sensible bid for the job. The group with the lowest reasonable bid will receive the job!

Each of you has been given your own individual tasks along with instructions for the completion of those tasks. There are charts in each of your folders where your work is to be recorded. Check your math carefully and show all of your work. Once you have completed your part, complete the *Bid Calculations* form (see figure 4.1, p. 57).

The goal of this project is to demonstrate mastery of the skills learned in the geometry chapter along with mastery of basic computational skills. This is your chance to put it all together and truly understand what carpenters do daily. Good Luck!

Although the group is working on one overall assignment, individual tasks vary from folder to folder. Each student is given specific tasks that must be completed before a bid on the job can be submitted (see figure 4.2, p. 58). Each job is dependent upon the others for its success. Cooperation is critical.

The activity commences. Mrs. Thomas serves mainly as a facilitator and informal assessor where she is free to assist and give attention as it is needed.

Variations

1. Groups might be determined according to readiness levels, where assignments could be tiered: high, medium-high, medium-low, and low.

2. Each group might be given a different assignment. Groups might present to the class.

3. Groups might be formulated according to interests or Learning Styles.

The Bottom Line

This lesson was engaging and meaningful to the students. It addressed individual differences in regard to ability, personality, and Multiple Intelligences. It allowed students to utilize knowledge gained in a real-life application, which is precisely what brings meaning and fosters in-depth understanding.

Figure 4.1
Bid Calculations

Information Needed	Fill in Below
Total square footage of room	
Dimensions of windows and doors	
Additional structures within the room	
Amount of time allocated for job completion	
Approximate date of completion	
	Costs
Total cost of materials (attach detailed list)	
Total delivery charges	
Labor charges	
Total Costs	
Contractor's Fee	
Final Bid	

Figure 4.2
Tasks

1. Madison (blue folder):

- Determine the area and perimeter of the room.

- Contact various builders and determine the cost of labor per square foot and approximate amount of time needed for completion.

- Obtain labor costs for additional structures that will be added to the room (shelves, wall units, computer centers, etc.). Consult with Bailey to obtain those measurements.

2. Paul (green folder):

- Measure windows and doors. Consult with Madison so that actual wall space can be determined.

- Compile a list of materials needed for the job.

- Assist Bailey in researching the costs of materials.

3. Simone (yellow folder):

- Consult with Paul and Madison in regard to the measurements. Then determine the amounts of each material that will be needed.

- Prepare a presentation using technology. (This will be presented to the class as the submission for the bid.)

4. Bailey (red folder):

- Determine dimensions of the additional structures in the room and present those to Madison who will obtain the costs of building those structures.

- Consult with Simone to determine necessary materials and amounts of each that will be needed, then research the costs of those materials at various stores. Include delivery charges.

- Construct handouts for the class. Consult with Simone to coordinate the handouts with the presentation.

2

Jigsaw Puzzles

I'm puzzled by the students' lack of energy and drive
I'm puzzled by the look of apathy in every eye
I'm disconcerted, saddened, and offended by their moods
And angered when they're impolite or simply downright rude.

I'm puzzled by their nonchalance toward everything I say
Perplexed by looks of boredom every one of them displays
With each look of confusion and frustration they exude
I plead for an adjustment to their ghastly attitudes.

But all of my imploring didn't garner any fervor
The blaming and accusing seemed to distance students further
The reason that the pieces of the puzzle hadn't fit
Was looking squarely at me in the mirror, I was it!

—Elizabeth Breaux

What Are They?

A conventional jigsaw puzzle is typically thought to be complete (or solved) when the individual pieces fit or come together to create a whole. As long as the individual parts are not yet occupying their proper places, thereby completing their "jobs as part of the big picture," the puzzle is unfinished. A jigsaw puzzle is a potential "whole" broken into pieces that are waiting to become whole again!

When using Jigsaw Puzzles as a method of instruction, the assumption is that the students have little or no prior knowledge of a particular topic; students are placed in groups BEFORE instruction occurs (as opposed to Cooperative Grouping activities where direct instruction is a prerequisite). Jigsaw Puzzles are student-directed and require that each student research something new, a separate piece of the puzzle, then return to the group and teach the other members.

Let's consider a science class where the chosen topic of study is *The Life Cycle of a Butterfly*. The teacher has chosen this topic for study but wants the students to self-direct the activity. The teacher might utilize the Jigsaw Puzzles method by dividing the class into several groups of 4 members each. The topic of study, *The Life Cycle of a Butterfly* in this case, would be divided into 4 sub-topics or "pieces," ensuring that each group member researches a single area.

Topic—*The Life Cycle of a Butterfly*

Sub-topics:
1. Egg
2. Larva
3. Pupa
4. Butterfly

If the teacher's class consists of 20 students, a total of 5 groups with 4 members each would be formed. Each student would be given one piece (in this case, one stage of the butterfly's life cycle) to study, research, etc. Once individual students complete their research/assignments, each individual group member would meet with members of the other groups who had been assigned the same stage of the butterfly's life cycle. In other words, 5 new groups would be formed so that all students within the class, working on the same sub-topic (stage of the life cycle in this case), would be able to meet and share their findings. This allows students to collect information from others who are working on the same sub-topic, thereby enhancing their own find-ings before returning to their original groups. At this point they have become "mini experts" on their particular stage of the life cycle and are ready to teach their part to the rest of their group. Once each group member has taught his/her part to the rest of the group members, the group will have the information necessary to complete the project/assignment on the topic: *The Life Cycle of a Butterfly.*

Following are some steps to follow when creating a jigsaw puzzle activity for your class:

1. Determine the topic of study and the objective(s).

2. Divide the topic into several (4–5) important sub-topics or "pieces."

3. Create an activity, assignment, etc., for each piece. Be specific!

   Suggestion: Write each activity and its details on an index card. Number the index cards according to sub-topics (i.e. 1, 2, 3, and 4). Each group should have identical sets of cards.

4. Devise a rubric for grading each component, and another for grading the overall final product.

5. Divide students into groups.

6. Allow students to meet with their group members. At this time the teacher can either assign sub-topics (pieces) of study to individual students or allow students to randomly select them.

7. Discuss the project and the rubrics, along with all rules, procedures, logistics, etc., and then begin the activity/assignment.

8. After students complete their individual research on their sub-topics (pieces), they will meet with members of the other groups who have been working on the same sub-topics (pieces). (Since the assignment/index cards were numbered, simply have all like numbers meet together in new groups.)

9. Each student will share his/her information with the others while gathering new facts from the others. (The teacher will meet with each group to verify that the information being shared is factual.)

10. Students will then rejoin their original groups. They have become "mini experts" who will present their findings to the group. (Group members should be encouraged to ask questions for complete understanding.)

11. At this time the groups might be asked to present their findings to the class as a whole, or the teacher might circulate from group to group asking questions. Regardless of the method used, a predetermined rubric should be utilized for final assessment.

Classroom Scenario

As part of Black History Month at Northside High, the students in Mr. Marcel's history class have chosen to write a biography entitled *The Life of Barack Obama,* which will be presented during the celebration. This undertaking will require that a vast amount of research be conducted. Because time is a factor, students will have to work together. Because his students are competitive by nature, Mr. Marcel decides to use the Jigsaw Puzzles method, in which the class will be subdivided into several groups. Each group will create its own biography. The best one will be presented by the winning group during the assembly.

The Differentiated Way

Planning

Because this is a competition, Mr. Marcel wants to create groups that are similar in nature. He knows that he will create 6 five-member teams/groups. He constructs the groups so that each is balanced in regard to levels of ability, from low to high.

Mr. Marcel divides the topic into five sub-topics (pieces of Barack Obama's life) that will be addressed in detail in each group's biography.

1. Childhood

2. Education and College Years

3. Life as a Congressman

4. Family Life

5. Road to the Presidency

He constructs the following:

- assignment cards
- rules and procedures for the activity
- an outline for the biography (see figure 4.3, p. 65)
- rubrics to accompany each sub-topic
- a rubric to assess the final product (biography)
- timeline for the activity

- logistical plan for using research materials
- written assessment

The entire Jigsaw Puzzles process will be divided into phases that will culminate in one final product when the pieces come together to complete the puzzle.

Phase 1: Students in each group will conduct independent research on their individual sub-topics (pieces).

Phase 2: Students with like sub-topics from each group will meet to share findings.

Phase 3: Students will return to their original groups where they will use the information they have gathered to teach other group members. The teacher will circulate asking questions to ensure that the information is accurate and is being absorbed.

Phase 4: The groups will compile all information from all sub-topics and construct one biography.

He obtains several biographies (on various people) written by groups from years past. He will use these as samples of final products. He prepares the room in advance.

Implementation

As students enter the room, each is given a colored card (indicating group assignment). A number is also written on each card indicating specific individual assignments (sub-topics and directions) within the group. Desks have already been grouped. A colored flag has been placed within each group so that students can easily find their groups once handed the colored card at the door.

He proceeds with his explanation of the project, during which time he explains the following:

- rules and procedures for the activity
- the outline of the final product
- the specifics of each rubric
- a logistical plan for conducting research at various research centers (library, computer lab, classroom computers, classroom magazine and newspaper section, etc.)

He assigns sub-topics based on the number on the card that each child has received:

   #1 Childhood

   #2 Education and College Years

   #3 Life as a Congressman

   #4 Family Life

   #5 Road to the Presidency

Next, he explains the four Phases of the assignment to the students and the activity commences. The following is what occurs during each phase:

Phase 1: Students conduct research at various centers where they obtain the necessary information. Mr. Marcel facilitates, monitors and informally assesses.

Phase 2: Students with like sub-topics/same numbered cards meet to share their findings and to gather additional information from one another. Mr. Marcel visits the sessions in progress to determine accuracy of information being shared.

Phase 3: Students return to their original groups where they take turns teaching the rest of the group. Again Mr. Marcel monitors or informally assesses each group from time to time, asking relevant questions that will help him to determine the effectiveness of the teaching that is occurring within each group.

Phase 4: Groups use the outline to complete one group biography.

Upon completion of the biographies, Mr. Marcel scores each using the predetermined rubric. He administers a written test to all students. He uses the scores from both of these to establish a winning team.

Variations

1. Use for inter-curricular projects where several disciplines come together to work toward a common goal. Each class can be given its own part. Groups could then be formed by combining members of all classes. This is an excellent way to incorporate "Team Teaching" (see Chapter 4, #12).

2. Use with any discipline and/or topic to teach/promote team-building.

3. Use in a class of varying abilities, readiness, etc.

   Example: In a class of 24, you may have eight groups of three students each. Assign two or three different Jigsaw Puzzles at once. All Jigsaw Puzzles should relate to the same topic, but may be on varying levels of complexity. Color coding and numbering would allow for smooth transitions.

4. Consider grouping students according to Multiple Intelligences.

The Bottom Line

Jigsaw Puzzles are excellent for promoting teamwork and encouraging self-directed instruction. They place the responsibility for learning on the shoulders of the students. In this way, they encourage team-building and foster self-esteem. Because each individual in each group is given a different piece of the puzzle to complete, tasks can be tailored to meet specific needs of students. Due to the self-directed nature of Jigsaw Puzzles, the teacher is availed the opportunity to provide individualized attention and instruction as needed.

Figure 4.3

Outline for Biography

I.   Paragraph 1: Introduction
II.   Paragraph 2: Childhood
III. Paragraph 3: Education and College Years
IV.   Paragraph 4: Life as a Congressman
V.   Paragraph 5: Family Life
VI.   Paragraph 6: Road to the Presidency
VII. Closing/Culminating paragraph

3
Centers

So much to do, so much to learn
So many points for me to earn
One hundred ways for me to try it
(I am intrigued, I can't deny it)
A few are vague, but most are clear
The odds are in my favor here
With class work cloaked in such disguise
My learning can't be compromised!

—Elizabeth Breaux

What Are They?

Centers are basically stations created around the instructional setting, where different tasks are to be accomplished. All tasks can be related to one concept or they can be completely independent of one another. Centers can be used for small groups or for students working independently. Their implementation can be based on a "clockwork" concept, where groups move from one center (or station) to another with precision (where timing is specified), or where individuals move arbitrarily in accordance with particular needs and where timing is not of great importance.

Centers can be used within a general classroom setting, in an outdoor setting, or in any setting for that matter. Try using them at home with your children by creating Centers around the home where specific in-home cleaning duties will occur. Rotate children from center to center until the entire house is clean! Invite the neighbor's children. Make it fun! (**Warning**: We have not attempted this, so results cannot be guaranteed.)

The number of Centers created for every lesson will depend on the number and specific needs of the students. It will also depend, of course, on the physical layout and size of the workspace. The activities slated for each center are in direct accordance with the needs of the individual, the concepts being addressed, and the goals and objectives for the classroom.

Classroom Scenario

Call us crazy, but we are so intrigued by our idea for "House-Cleaning Centers" that we are going to use it as one of our examples! Because we are such proponents of real-life teaching and learning, we believe that the two are always much more closely related than they appear. As teachers we must always keep in mind that the more we relate classroom activities for learning to real-life activities for learning (see Chapter 4, #11), the more successful our students will be. So, in this "classroom" scenario, we will venture into the home of Mrs. Brown.

Mrs. Brown is a ninth-grade math teacher who has two young sons and one young daughter. None enjoy doing their household chores, but all enjoy receiving their allowances each Saturday. Mrs. Brown has always believed that children should be raised to understand that nothing in life is free. Possibilities are endless, but we must work for all that we acquire.

Because Mrs. Brown is quite the creative person, she has contrived another unique and intriguing approach to getting her children to earn their week's allowance. She will take the Differentiated Instruction activity that she plans to use next week with her students and adapt it so that it can be used inside of her home with her own children. With her classroom learning centers in mind, she will create a differentiated house-cleaning activity comprised of House-Cleaning Centers!

The Differentiated Way

Planning

Mrs. Brown begins working on the details of the lesson/activity. She knows that meticulous planning always leads to successful implementation in her classroom, so she aspires to do the same with this in-home activity.

First, Mrs. Brown considers the objectives for the lesson:

1. The children will demonstrate without assistance the ability to perform specific household tasks, which will be measured on a checklist for completion of tasks and degree of cleanliness.

2. The children will develop an appreciation of household cleanliness that will be measured by increased cleanliness in the house.

Next, she considers her three children. What are their strengths and weaknesses? What are their individual likes and dislikes? What motivates each?

Finally, Mrs. Brown considers the tasks at hand in more specific terms (in regard to what is to be accomplished):

1. vacuum

2. dust

3. clean kitchen

4. mop floors

5. clean bathrooms

Armed with the information necessary to plan an effective differentiated lesson, Mrs. Brown commences designing the activity:

1. She finds a box into which she will place the details of the various house-cleaning chores (written on individual task cards).

2. She creates the task cards by writing the following information on note cards and places them into the box:
   - Front side: description of chore
   - Back side: rubric that details expectations and amount of points that can be earned at varying levels of proficiency.

3. She creates a score card for each child. Each point earned will be the equivalent of $1.00 in allowance money.

4. She makes a list of all materials and supplies that will be needed to complete the tasks/activities.

5. She designs the instructional part of the lesson, where the necessary teaching will occur. She will reinforce and build upon previously learned skills in order to introduce and teach new skills.

6. She makes a list of the rules and procedures that will accompany the activity.

7. She determines her own duties in the implementation:
   - teach/review
   - monitor
   - guide
   - reinforce/reteach
   - assess

NOTE: She WILL NOT be partaking in the actual cleaning!

Implementation

On Tuesday evening, Mrs. Brown announces to the children that they are to be ready at 9:00 a.m. on Saturday to earn their allowances for the week. She does not go into detail but does entice them by disclosing that they will have the opportunity to earn more than the usual weekly allowance. She "dangles the carrot" a little each day after that in an attempt to further pique their curiosities. (She enjoys this part immensely!)

At 8:00 a.m. on Saturday Mrs. Brown gathers all materials and supplies. She places the box of task cards on the kitchen table. She lays out three score cards, one for each child. Next to each is a page detailing the rules and procedures that will guide the activity.

At 9:00 a.m. she gathers the children around the table, hands out the score cards, and begins to teach the lesson.

"First," says Mrs. Brown, "you should all know that you will have the opportunity to earn more than your usual allowance today. The amount that you earn will be up to you. You can earn as little as $00.00 or as much as $25.00."

She hands each child a score card and continues.

"By 12:00 noon, this activity will end. At that time you will be given $1.00 for each point earned. Here is how you will earn points."

She places the box of task cards in front of the children and instructs each to pull one card from the box. She refers to each child's card as she continues.

"I see that Andrew has just pulled the 'vacuum and dust the living room' card, which could earn as many as four points/dollars. Alexander has the 'clean the hallway bathroom' card which can earn as many as five points/dollars, and Ayden is holding the 'clean the kitchen' card, which can earn as many as six points/dollars. I know that Alexander hates to clean the bathroom and Ayden hates to clean the kitchen, so the two of you may swap cards if you would like.

"Another option would be to return the card to the box and pull another.

"You will only be able to choose one of these options each time you complete one task and draw a card for another, so know that by drawing another card you will be taking a chance at getting a task that is even less attractive to you than the previous one. A huge factor to consider is that the more difficult and less appealing the task/job, the higher the possible earnings!"

Ayden rolls her eyes and sucks her teeth in obvious disapproval of her mother's newly concocted idea for earning allowances. She is about to learn that the gestures just earned her negative points.

"Oh, that reminds me," says Mrs. Brown, "There are certain rules that, if broken, will result in a consequence. Please look at the 'rules and procedures' page. As you will notice, disrespect toward your mother carries a heavy penalty. Ayden has just demonstrated the fine art of losing one point/dollar."

Mrs. Brown changes the "0" on Ayden's score card to a "–1."

"That doesn't bother me," Ayden says in a sarcastic tone.

"–2 points" says Mrs. Brown. "As of right now you owe me $2.00. I would suggest that you start earning your allowance as opposed to spending it before you receive it."

Mrs. Brown now directs the children's attention to the task card.

"The directions, as to the specifications of your task, are clearly written. If the total possible points that can be earned for the task is 4, you must complete the task in its entirety and in accordance with the specifications on the rubric in order to earn the entire amount. When you have completed your task and are ready for me to assess it, you should ask for me to do so. At that time I will check your work, record your score, and instruct you to pick another task from the box. There are a total of 12 tasks in the box. We will stop when all have been completed, or at 12:00 noon, whichever comes first. At that time, scores will be tallied, points converted to dollars, and allowances given."

Mrs. Brown pulls all 12 task cards from the box and discusses each with the children. She takes them to all of the task areas (Centers) and, using the directions on the cards, teaches and reteaches the skills necessary for completing each task. Questions are asked and answered. Demonstrations are given. Supplies are provided. The activity begins.

The family returns to the table where sits the task box, the rules and procedures list, and the score cards. All children pick a task card from the box. Andrew picks a tough one, which could earn a large number of points. This one is challenging, but he is up for the challenge and begins his task. Alexander picks one that involves cleaning a toilet, and although the points are enticing he wants to exchange it. Ayden wants him to trade his for hers, but he does not like the one she has chosen, and so he chooses to return his to the box instead. Ayden becomes visibly upset and almost loses more points. She restrains herself and chooses to comply. (Her mother has already demonstrated that she intends to play by the rules and Ayden knows that she means it!) She decides to stick with the one she has chosen, and she begins the task. Alexander draws another task card, one that is more to his liking, and begins.

As the children complete each task, Mrs. Brown checks their work, gives feedback, and awards points. Another task card is then picked from the box, and the activity continues until all task cards have been taken from the box and tasks have been completed.

At 11:45 a.m. Mrs. Brown calls the children to the table, one at a time, for a private discussion regarding their individual accomplishments.

"Andrew, you managed to work quickly, yet efficiently. Of the 12 tasks that were in the box, you completed 5 and earned a total of 20 points or $20.00.

"Alexander, you were a little reluctant to complete some of the tasks, and although you did complete 4 of them, you did not complete all components as well as you could have. Out of a possible 23 points, you earned 16, or $16.00.

"Ayden, you did well once you stopped complaining and started working. You managed to complete 3 tasks for a total of 12 points. After factoring in the loss of the 2 points for rules infractions, your total comes to 10 points, or $10.00."

After handing out the money, Mrs. Brown asked the children for feedback. She was pleasantly surprised at what the children had to say. Although none of them enjoyed the house-cleaning, they enjoyed reaping the benefits. They felt as though they were in charge of their earnings. There was more of a sense of pride felt by all when their jobs were done well. They even added suggestions for future "House-Cleaning Centers" days, and Mrs. Brown wrote down the suggestions:

- Andrew suggested that more tasks be included in the task box and that the workers be given more time to complete them. He suggested that a wider variety of tasks be included, such as cleaning windows, blinds, appliances, etc.

- Alexander suggested that they sit together and choose their own tasks, so that way they would all know in advance what tasks they were to complete.

- Ayden suggested that they be given the entire week to complete tasks, and that the week should end on Friday afternoon. Thus, the option would allow them to be free on the weekends.

Mrs. Brown considered all suggestions and made amendments to the rules and procedures. Future plans will include teaching the children new tasks and helping them to become more efficient at the old ones.

That evening, Mrs. Brown shared the events of the day with her husband. He is now devising his own lessons where he will teach the children to paint, manicure the yard, fix leaky pipes, change the air conditioner filter, change the oil in the car, build a compost bin, and repair a broken fence. He figures that this would allow for a year's worth of his work to be completed in one weekend!

On Monday, Mrs. Brown takes this concept back into her classroom where she creates Learning Centers for her social studies classes. Each center will encompass a different aspect of the War of 1812. At each center, specific tasks will be completed. Task cards similar to those she used at home are prepared: Directions for completion are written on the front (see figure 4.4, p. 75) and either a scoring rubric or an explanation of how points can be earned is written on the back (see figure 4.5, p. 75). A score card is prepared for each student (see figure 4.6, p. 76 for a filled-in example).

Preparation and planning consist of the same steps that were used when creating the House-Cleaning Centers:

1. Defining the objectives.

2. Determining individual strengths and weaknesses and likes and dislikes of individual students.

3. Creating Centers that allow for the different aspects of the war to be studied using a variety of methods that address all learners.

4. Deciding whether students should work individually and at their own pace or in groups that rotate in tandem.

5. Determining the rules and procedures that will provide for efficient implementation of the activity (see figure 4.7, p. 76).

The lesson is implemented in much the same way as the House-Cleaning Centers were:

1. An introduction is given: distributing and explaining directions, grading rubrics, and score cards.

2. A guided tour is conducted to all Centers where the details of each activity are explained and questions are asked and answered.

3. Rules and procedures are clarified for the students.

Mrs. Brown's role during the implementation is again that of a monitor, facilitator, and assessor. At the completion of the activity, students are gathered and general feedback is given. Questions are asked and answered. Students are encouraged to give suggestions for future activities. Score cards are collected, points are tallied, and results are shared.

Variations

- Centers can be set up so that a complete rotation is achieved in as little as one class period or as much as a week or more, in which case every student would visit every center. Activities can be highly or minimally detailed.

- Students can be given the choice as to which Centers will be visited and which will not. Thus a greater number of Centers might be formed.

- Centers can be created with varying learning levels in mind and with activities that are more specific to students at those levels. In this case, students would be assigned to particular Centers.
- Centers can be created within the walls of one classroom, or they might encompass a broader spectrum where movement to other areas of the campus (library, computer lab, another teacher's classroom, etc.) is necessary.
- Centers work beautifully in a physical education class where many Centers can be created around the gymnasium or in a large outdoor space. Students engage in various physical activities at each center. The teacher can group students by ability level so that he/she can give more individual attention to those groups that might be struggling.

Be creative. The more creative the activity, the more enticing it will be to the students. Enticement leads to engagement, which leads to success! Mission accomplished!

The Bottom Line

There are few easier ways to differentiate than through the use of Centers, when consideration is given to the limitless possibilities they afford. Centers allow for varying of activities, tiered activities, individualizing attention where needed, reteaching as needed, formal and informal assessing, etc. The hard work comes in the preparation, but the implementation can be virtually stress-free while allowing for optimal efficiency and effectiveness. So get to work preparing Centers and get ready to reap the benefits!

Figure 4.4

These are the directions for implementation of a specific activity at a given center. These directions would be written on the front side of the card. (All supplies necessary for the implementation of this activity have been placed at the center by the teacher.)

(front side of card)

Center #1: Jeopardy Challenge

Directions: Read the twenty questions that have been provided for you on the activity sheet. Remove the twenty strips from the zippered bag. These strips are the answers to the questions on the activity sheet. Set the timer for five minutes. Place the correct answer strip next to its question. Complete as many as you can within the five-minute period.

Figure 4.5

This can be either a scoring rubric or an explanation as to how points are to be earned.

(back side of card)

A possible twenty points can be earned for this activity. Each correct match is worth one point.

Figure 4.6

Each child would be given his/her own individual score card, which when complete, would look something like this one.

Name:_____

Centers on The War of 1812

Center	Earned Points	Possible Points	Score
#1	3	4	3/4=75%
#2	5	5	5/5=100%
#3	18	20	18/20=90%
#4	8	10	8/10=80%
#5	15	15	15/15=100%
Totals	49	54	49/54=91%

Figure 4.7
Rules and Procedures for Centers on The War of 1812

1. *Students will begin at a given center designated by the teacher and will move to a new center upon the direction of the teacher only. Movement away from designated Centers for other reasons is not allowed.
2. Centers are numbered from 1 to 5. Rotation will be in numerical order. Groups leaving Center #5 will move next to Center #1.
3. *Students will work in groups of four. Communication between group members is allowed, but communication with members of different groups is not.
4. Any student needing assistance should place the red flag in its stand. This will alert the teacher that assistance is needed.
5. Upon completion of the assigned activities, students should place the green flag in its stand. This will alert the teacher who will check and score the completed work.

*Denotes a rule which carries a consequence if broken. One point will be subtracted from the score card for each and every infraction.

4
Tiered Assignments

Towers begin with foundations
With groundwork the critical part
A life is not lived to its fullest extent
If it doesn't evolve from the heart.

The heart of a life is its soul
And the source of all light is the sun
Problems can't multiply void of a root
Since the basis of many is one.

A ship needs a sea to embark on
Man needs a world to explore
Perceptions need glimpses so that to be seen
While rockets need launches to soar.

Beginnings need breath blown into them
Fires need sparks to ignite
Children need teachers to channel their paths
Their futures won't shine without light.

—Elizabeth Breaux

What Are They?

The ultimate goal of any lesson is to create an optimal classroom experience for all learners. "Optimal" for one student, however, might prove least favorable for another. Students come to us with varying backgrounds and abilities. They each have personal and educational experiences. Yet we are expected to teach them all with the same objectives and goals. How do we accomplish such great feats?

Success begins with a strong foundation. In the classroom, the type of foundation that is laid is determined by first accessing the students' prior knowledge of the subject matter. Imagine a staircase when considering students' knowledge base. Many students come to us with solid foundations, but are on different steps of the staircase. Others come with weak foundations that need additional supports before steps can be laid. We must ensure that solid foundations are in place for all students so they can climb the staircase, one step at a time, and achieve success at each level/step along the way.

Teachers should begin any lesson by probing students to access their prior knowledge of a skill or subject matter. Make this process fun and engaging for students because it will lay the foundation of your lesson. Consider doing one or more of the following:

1. Brainstorm information about the topic. List the information on a chart or board and leave the information up throughout the duration of the lesson.

2. Complete a chart on what students know and what students would like to know about a topic.

3. Relate the topic to something with which the students can identify in their everyday life.

Example A: Give all students a potato chip and ask them to look at the chip and list its characteristics. Then ask them to taste the chip and list some additional characteristics. Create a list of all words used to describe the chip and then introduce adjectives. This activity allows students to create a mental connection between the potato chip activity and the use of adjectives.

Example B: Give each student a bag of M&Ms. Ask the students to place the M&Ms around the outside of a circle. Allow students to count the number of M&Ms used. Once students are comfortable with this process, introduce circumference. This activity allows students to create a mental connection between the M&Ms activity and circumference.

Example C: You are about to have your students begin reading a novel in class. Before doing so, show students pictures and ask them to explain the details of the pictures. If the setting and events of the story take place in Alaska, bring different pictures of Alaska and discuss the ways of life in Alaska. Allow them to discuss the pictures; what they see and what inferences they can make. Then introduce the novel. As you discuss the novel in class, refer back to the pictures and information discussed in the pictures.

Example D: You are about to begin teaching a unit on the different types of clouds. Take the students on a field trip or scavenger hunt. This is an excellent way to engage students in the learning process. Allow them to draw the different clouds in the sky. Ask students to describe each cloud that is drawn. You may want to give students cotton balls to use in their pictures. Then introduce the lesson.

Example E: You are teaching students the parts of a flower. Allow them to go outside and collect flowers or have them bring them in from home. Discuss the different flowers and list their common characteristics. After prior knowledge is activated, begin the lesson.

1. For topics on which students have no background knowledge or information, begin with a bulletin board.

    Example: In two weeks, you will begin teaching a unit on cells. This is a new unfamiliar concept. Create a bulletin board. Do not place a title on the board. Instead, place a large circle in the middle of the board. As students come into class, they may question you or their classmates about the board. (This may not happen the first day, but give it time.) Do not answer any questions about the board. Keep it mysterious. Slowly add detail to your board. Remember as students ask about the untitled board keep it a mystery. Entice the students by giving them little details. This process will be occurring while you are teaching another topic. This is just side information and discussion. Pace yourself in order to finish the bulletin board around the same time as your lesson is scheduled to begin. Then introduce the new lesson. Students will have prior knowledge from seeing the bulletin board being created one step at a time.

The beginning of any lesson is an ideal time to reiterate all of the basic foundational knowledge that all students are expected to have. Continue the lesson by introducing students to the objective (s) of the day via modeling. This essential part of the lesson is where a strong, solid foundation is created. Offer the students various methods for processing and learning the skill. Allow students the opportunity to model the skill, after which they should be ready to transition into independent practice.

Before transitioning, however, consider the staircase: *Are all students on the same step?* In most classrooms, the answer is probably "no," in which case an optimal learning environment for all cannot be achieved by assigning all students the same independent practice activity. This is where Tiered Assignments come into play.

Tiered Assignments are similar assignments that allow all students to work on the same essential skill but at different levels of readiness and complexity. The purpose is to allow all students the opportunity to reach the same common goal but in their own individual ways. Tiered Assignments address this by altering the levels of complexity in order to accommodate for varying levels of readiness.

NOTE: *Readiness level* is a student's current state of knowledge in respect to a particular subject.

Complexity level is the level of difficulty in regard to a specific task.

When creating Tiered Assignments, one must first determine the ultimate goal of the lesson. Create one assignment/activity that would allow for the "average" students to demonstrate their current knowledge level of the topic while slightly challenging them to enhance that current level. The activity should be challenging, but not so difficult that it cannot be completed independently.

Once this "average" assignment has been completed, use it as a guide to create assignments for the more advanced students and for the more challenged students. Special attention should be paid to the levels of complexity of the assignments and to the levels of readiness of the individual students. All assignments should be similar in time requirements for completion. In other words, the more advanced students would not necessarily have more work to complete, but instead would be given more complex work. By the same token, the lower-level students would not be given less work, but instead would be given less complex work.

NOTE: It is important to expose all students to the same foundational instruction before proceeding to more individualized Tiered Assignments.

The objective for Mr. Sims' math lesson was that *the students will be able to add fractions with unlike denominators.* In the initial phases of the lesson, Mr. Sims probed students to ascertain their prior knowledge on addition of fractions. At that time, he was able to determine that most students were on average levels of readiness (for their age and grade level) in relation to this particular skill. Two of his students had no prior knowledge base, and another two were already familiar with the skill and ready to be challenged.

Because two of his students did not possess the basic foundational knowledge necessary to be ready to learn to add fractions with unlike denominators, he had to find a way to provide them with the necessary remediation. Because the two students were already enrolled in the after-school tutoring program, he arranged to work with them that afternoon and was able to increase their readiness levels. The next day, Mr. Sims was able to continue the lesson (with the entire class) by modeling the skill in a variety of ways. He provided guided practice and was relatively certain that all students were ready to move into the independent practice phase of the lesson.

Before proceeding to the independent practice, Mr. Sims had to plan activities that took varying readiness levels into consideration.

The Differentiated Way

Planning

Mr. Sims proceeded to plan three separate assignments/activities, all of which accounted for levels of readiness with specific attention to levels of complexity.

NOTE: The activities we will use in the examples are created on three separate tiers, but additional tiers are always an option that should be considered. There is no magic number for the number of tiers in an assignment.

1. Assignment for *Average* Students:

   Objective: The learner will add fractions with unlike denominators.
   Assignment: Students will solve 15 problems with unlike denominators. All answers must be reduced to their least common denominators. Eleven of the problems will require adding two fractions with unlike denominators ranging from 1 to 20. Three problems will require adding three fractions with unlike denominators ranging from 1 to

20. One problem will require deciphering a word problem in which unlike denominators, ranging from 1 to 20, must be added.

2. Assignment for *Advanced* Students:

   Objective: The learner will add fractions with unlike denominators. Assignment: Students will solve 8 word problems, all of which consist of two to three fractions with unlike denominators ranging from 1 to 20. All answers must be reduced to the least common denominator.

3. Assignment for *Lower-Level* Students:

   Objective: The learner will add fractions with unlike denominators. Assignment: Students will solve 10 problems with unlike denominators. Five problems will require adding two fractions with unlike denominators ranging from 1 to 10. Three problems will require adding three fractions with unlike denominators ranging from 1 to 10. Two problems will require adding two fractions with unlike denominators ranging from 1 to 20. Students may use manipulatives to complete the tasks. All answers do not have to be reduced to the least common denominator.

The objective, *The learner will add fractions with unlike denominators*, is the same for all students. All students will be required to demonstrate their knowledge of the skill. Lower-level students will be able to complete less complex problems before they advance toward more difficult problems. In addition, they will be allowed to use their manipulatives to aid their learning. On the other hand, the higher-level students will be required to complete more complex word problems, which will require the use of analytical thinking skills and the ability to synthesize the information.

Implementation

The next day, Mr. Sims completed a quick review of the skill via question/answer and modeling sessions. Upon completion of the two, he immediately transitioned the lesson into the independent practice phase by giving each student the predetermined, appropriately-tiered assignment. As he had expected, the two weaker students needed the most individual attention, which he was able to provide while the others worked on their own Tiered Assignments.

Variations

1. Develop a project with multiple components. Components should be assigned in accordance with levels of readiness. This allows all students to be involved in creating the final project.
2. Create three or four completely different projects related to the same topic. Level the projects according to complexity. Design them so that each requires a comparable amount of time for completion.

There is no set number of Tiered Assignments to develop. Try to shoot for three or four. Start small and increase the number depending on the levels of your students.

The Bottom Line

Before assigning independent practice, place your students on the staircase to success. First, make certain that all possess a well-laid structure/support. Then, build the steps. Create assignments that are "step (tier)-appropriate." When creating Tiered Assignments, remember that you must change the complexity of the material at each step in order to ensure success. This challenges students "where they are," before moving them toward "where they need to be." The key is to challenge students, not to give them more of the same material.

5
Progressive Pockets

If Peter Piper had the chance to play "Progressive Pockets"
And saw that learning could be fun he probably wouldn't knock it
Instead he'd venture further, with curious intentions
And ask the questions that before would never have been mentioned.
"How is this done? I'd like to know, and really like to try it!
It makes me think and use my hands; if it wasn't free I'd buy it!
It's fun and even though it's 'work' I'd never call it boring
Like the lesson we had yesterday that moved us all to snoring!"

— *Elizabeth Breaux*

What Are They?

Progressive Pockets are precisely what they imply… they are pockets (either manila folders stapled on three sides or large envelopes work best) filled with "goodies" (activities) waiting to be "progressed" through. They can be used as the focal exercise of any lesson and/or used as enrichment or tutorial activities.

More simply put, they are leveled activities grouped together in individually leveled folders. A class with three fairly distinct learning levels (low, medium, high) would require that the activities be grouped in three distinct folders. Students, of course, are unaware that they are grouped according to learning levels. This can be achieved by simply assigning each student a number or letter (1, 2, 3 or A, B, C) and directing them to pick from the folder that coincides with the assigned number or letter. Each folder should include an ample number of activities that are hands-on, real-life oriented, and engaging.

Progressive Pockets can be used as individual or as group activities. Once students have successfully completed some or all of the activities in the initially assigned "pockets," they can progress to the more difficult, higher-leveled pockets. In addition, Progressive Pockets can be utilized when additional activities are needed for students who have completed a given assignment, for students who need additional reinforcement of a skill, or simply as "extra points" activities.

Classroom Scenario

The alternative education class is comprised of students who are all performing below grade level. Students range in age from 13 to 16. Most are very poor readers and writers. The state exam, which is given in April, requires that students write a 200-word essay. Many of these students are struggling to write complete sentences. A few are able to write semi-structured paragraphs, but none are able to write well-structured extended pieces.

For years, Ms. Gomez tried to fight her way out of this quandary of insisting they write essays when they were incapable of doing so. She finally realized she must meet them where they are and make them successful at that level before she could move them forward.

The Differentiated Way

Planning

Ms. Gomez created several hands-on writing activities and placed each into one of five grouping levels: A (low level), B (intermediate level), C (high level), D (advanced level), E (enrichment level). She used large manila folders, stapled on three sides creating pockets, to house these activities. On the cover of each was written the letter of the level (A, B, C, D, E). She created 10 activities for each pocket. As with all hands-on activities, attention to detail in the planning phase made the activities more enticing to the students. Ms. Gomez made certain that each folder was complete with the following:

1. **completion cards**: One of these was created for each activity. The cards were used to keep a record of students who had completed each activity within the pocket. This ensured that students completed a given activity only once (see figure 4.8, p. 90).

2. **individual activity bags:** Ten of these were included in each pocket, each holding a separate activity (see figure 4.11, p. 91). (Zippered bags work best. Each zippered activity bag should be labeled with the name of the activity and the pocket [A, B, C, D, E] to which it belongs and to where it must be returned). A directions card (#3 below) should be included in each zippered bag along with all manipulatives needed for the activity.

3. **directions cards**: Each activity (total of 10 per pocket) in the pocket should include its own set of directions (see figures 4.9 and 4.10, pp. 90–91).

If the teacher chooses to make this a graded activity, individual **score sheets** should be given to each student in advance and collected at the end of each session (see figure 4.12, p. 92). These should not be included in the pockets, because this information is not for all to see.

NOTE: All activity items should be laminated so that the initial work on the part of the teacher is done during the first year of usage only. Lamination ensures that the activities can "live" in their pockets until they are taken from hibernation in future years.

Place a variety of different activities in each folder. The more the better! Add to the activities each year. Remove those that have proven least effective and replace them with new ones. Label all folders or envelopes with the proper lessons/standards/subjects/topics to which they coincide and file them away in alphabetical order so that they are easily accessible in the future. That's it!

Implementation

For this particular lesson, Ms. Gomez chooses to use the Progressive Pockets as an individualized activity. She has already determined the various ability levels of her students (in relation to writing) and has a predetermined list of the level at which each student will begin.

Before the class enters the room, Ms. Gomez places all of the previously prepared pockets in the front of the room where they can be easily seen and referred to during her initial explanation of the activity. All are labeled with a letter (A, B, C, D, E). Each pocket contains 10 activities. Because Ms. Gomez has chosen to grade the activities, she has created for each student an individual score sheet, which will be given to the students during the explanation of the activity. Ms. Gomez explains the procedure to the students. She assigns each student a letter, which coincides with what she has predetermined to be their beginning pocket level. This predetermination of levels is as follows:

- A (low) = seven students
- B (intermediate) = eight students
- C (high) = five students
- D (advanced) = none
- E (enrichment) = none

Students are called upon, three or four at a time, to approach the pockets and pick one activity, each from the assigned pocket, before returning to their seats. Ms. Gomez distributes the score sheets, one per student (see figure 4.12, p. 92). She explains the procedure that will be used in the implementation of the activity:

1. Each student is to write his/her name on the score sheet. She explains that each activity has been given a predetermined amount of possible points that can be earned and she refers to each on the score sheet. As students complete an activity, they are to alert her so that she can score and award points before allowing students to return the activity bag to its proper pocket for use by another student.

   NOTE: Make certain that the date column on the score sheet is filled in for each activity completed on a particular day.

2. Students are to open their activity bags and read the directions. Any questions in reference to the directions will be answered before proceeding.

3. Once students have completed an activity and have had it checked and scored, they are to return the activity bag to the proper pocket and pick another activity from the same pocket.

   NOTE: If at any time during the activity the teacher determines that the current pocket level is not the most appropriate one, it should be changed.

Students are now asked to begin the activities. Ms. Gomez monitors and assists as needed. She corrects any improper implementation immediately so as to remain consistent. As students complete each level, they experience a sense of accomplishment and success. Off-task behaviors are seldom an issue.

Ms. Gomez allows one hour for the day's activities. She ends the activity five minutes before the bell rings in order to have time for all activity bags to be returned to the proper pockets and to collect all score sheets.

When tallying scores, Ms. Gomez first determines the amount of possible points that could have been earned by each student as indicated on the score sheet. She determines a percentage score based on the number of points earned divided by the number of possible points that could have been earned on the activity. Example: eight points earned out of ten possible points = 80%.

NOTE: The Progressive Pockets are utilized on upcoming days. As students successfully complete all activities in one pocket, they move on to the next level. This is detailed in the score sheet, see figure 4.12, p. 92.

Variations

Progressive Pockets can also be utilized for:

- Cooperative Grouping activities. (If used for Cooperative Grouping the activities would need to be tailored to fit the Cooperative Grouping profile; see Chapter 4, #1).
- remediation/tutorials.
- enrichment.
- activities for early finishers.

The Bottom Line

Progressive Pockets allow students to progress at their own level. Each level is built upon the previous level. Because success breeds success, future successes are imminent. Because students are given the opportunity to experience success, off-task behaviors are seldom an issue. The hands-on activities encourage student engagement. The teacher's constant involvement (monitoring, assisting, reteaching, scoring, encouraging) also helps keep students on task at all times. Because students are working independently, the teacher can give attention where it is needed most.

Figure 4.8
Completion Card

This is the card for **Pocket A, Activity Bag A–2**. The teacher will mark "complete" on the card before allowing a student to return the bag to retrieve a new one.

Completion Card for A–2

name	complete
Adams, Diane	√
Anders, David	
Brown, Yvette	√
Chargois, Louise	
Couch, Simone	
Dennis, Jaxon	
Hayes, Harrison	√

Figure 4.9
Directions Card for Pocket C, Activity Bag C–3

Directions for Activity C–3

Remove the 17 sentence strips from the zippered bag.
Divide them by color into three stacks (blue, red, green). These are the three paragraphs of a multi-paragraph essay.

Determine which sentence is the topic sentence for each and place it at the top of each stack. Next, determine which sentences would be the details for the paragraph and place them in their proper order. Once all three paragraphs have been arranged on your desktop, determine the proper order of the three paragraphs and arrange as such, so that the entire essay is in its proper order. Raise your hand upon completion.

Figure 4.10

Directions Card: This card lives inside of **Pocket A, Activity Bag A–2**.

Directions for Activity A–2

Remove the 10 sentence strips from the bag. Five of these are complete sentences. The other five are sentence fragments. Make two columns on your desk, one for the complete sentences and one for the incomplete sentences (or fragments). Raise your hand when you have completed the activity.

Figure 4.11

This is the outside of an **individual (zippered) activity bag** with label for **A–2**. The directions card and all components of the activity "live" inside.

A–2
Complete Sentences and Sentence Fragments

Figure 4.12

This is the individual **score sheet** of a student who has progressed from Level **A** through Level **C**.

Score Sheet

Name_____

Level/ Activity Bag #	Points Earned	Possible Points	Date Completed	% Score
A–1	4	5	8–30	80%
A–2	10	10	8-30	100%
A–3	7	8	8–30	88%
A–4	4	4	9–1	100%
A–5	5	5	9–1	100%
A–6	8	8	9–1	100%
A–7	8	10	9–1	80%
A–8	6	8	9–1	75%
A–9	8	10	9–10	80%
A–10	2	4	9–10	50%
B–1	5	6	9–10	83%
B-2	10	10	9–10	100%
B–3	8	10	9–10	80%
B–4	6	8	9–12	75%
B–5	10	10	9–12	100%
B–6	4	5	9–15	80%
B–7	10	10	9–15	100%
B–8	7	8	9–15	88%
B-9	4	4	9-28	100%
B-10	5	5	9-28	100%
C–1	8	8	9-28	100%
C–2	8	10	10-2	80%
C–3	6	8	10–2	75%
C–4	8	10	10–2	80%
C–5	2	4	10–4	50%
C–6	5	6	10–4	83%
C–7	10	10	10–6	100%
C–8	8	10	10–6	80%
C–9	6	8	10–11	75%
C–10	10	10	10–11	100%
Final Score	202	232		202/232=87%

6
Curriculum Compacting

My teacher said to practice, for perfect it would make
I followed her directive and examined my mistakes
I rehearsed until I could excel at every task
I outdid myself and all the others I surpassed.

My gears were switching smoothly, my engine running fine
My sights were set on destinations further down the line
There was no turning back now, no running out of steam
The prize ahead was one that I intended to redeem.

Then the teacher waved the flag, she stopped me in my tracks
Informed me I had gone too far, advised me to hold back
She said that I should wait for all the others to draw near
But what am I supposed to do while I am standing here?

—Elizabeth Breaux

What Is It?

There is nothing more frustrating to a well-prepared teacher than to hear the words, "This is boring!" These three little words can quickly reduce our hard efforts to nothingness. Our feelings of disillusionment lead to anger, which in turn directs us to admonish the offender, thereby turning him/her off even more. We resume the teaching of the lesson... the "boring" one. The cycle continues.

The cycle can be broken, but it is our job to recognize the need to disrupt it. To do that we must be willing to consider that boredom occurs for one of two reasons:

1. The learner has already mastered the information.

or

2. The learner does not possess enough information on the topic to generate any interest in the topic (on his/her own).

Unfortunately, enduring hours and hours of boredom is commonplace for some students. The ramifications can be many. Some simply lose interest in the learning process altogether. Others engage in off-task behaviors that require disciplinary interventions. At worst, some drop out of school.

Curriculum Compacting is a way for students, who demonstrate mastery in one area, to accelerate at their own pace. It affords students the opportunity to move through the curriculum at a quicker pace giving them the opportunity to concentrate on a more enriched and in-depth area of study in lieu of basic skills or drill and practice. The purpose of Curriculum Compacting is threefold:

1. Avoid reteaching of skills that have been previously mastered.

2. Eliminate boredom in high-achieving students.

3. Provide continuous growth.

Curriculum Compacting recognizes that students have individual needs. The goal is to eliminate the need for repeated drill and practice for those who do not need it. Many students can grasp a concept and retain the information more quickly than others and do not need the continuous review and repetition.

There are two types of Curriculum Compacting.

- Basic skills compacting: Basic skills compacting involves assessing all students to determine mastery of the basics: spelling, math computations, basic language arts skills, etc. The goal is to eliminate the need for redundant repetition or drill and practice for students who have already mastered the material.

- Content compacting: Content compacting allows students to move through the course content at their own speed. Some students need little assistance because they either have prior knowledge of the subject matter or they can master the material in a fraction of the time. These students should not be stifled in their learning process by being made to wait upon other students to catch up.

Curriculum Compacting takes into account that once mastery has occurred, students should progress. Logic tells us that this should be the case in all facets of the learning process, yet it is often overlooked in our classrooms. In the real world, our ability to think more rationally leads us in a different direction.

In the real world we intuitively know that it makes good sense to terminate the teaching of a particular skill once mastery has been achieved. We know this as a fact and would not question it. We would never continue insisting that a child practice reciting the alphabet once he/she is able to read a novel. We would never place the training wheels back onto the bike of a child who has learned to ride without them, simply for the sake of "practice." Imagine the frustration that would be endured by a husband who has just finished manicuring the lawn and is asked by his wife to do it again, one more time, just for practice!

Curriculum Compacting is a way to bring that same real life method of teaching into our classrooms. It is based on the premise that a student's growth and progress should not be impeded simply because he/she has already mastered a skill that others have not.

Renzulli and Smith's Curriculum Compacting Model includes the following steps:

1. Select the learning objectives for a given subject.

2. Find or create an appropriate way to pretest or to alternately assess competencies related to the objectives and determine a score or result that equates to mastery.

3. Identify students who may have mastered the objectives or have the potential to master them at a faster-than-normal pace.

4. Pretest those identified students before beginning instruction on one or more of the objectives. Pretesting all students is also an option.

5. Streamline practice, drill, or instructional time for students who have met the objectives.

6. Provide instructional options for students who have not yet attained all the pretested objectives, but generally learn faster than their classmates.

7. Organize and recommend enrichment or acceleration options for eligible students.

8. Keep records of the process and instructional options available to students whose curriculum has been compacted for reporting to parents and forward these records to next year's teachers.

If you are a novice at Curriculum Compacting, start small. In the real world we would never attempt to repair a vehicle's engine without first knowing how to change the oil. The same is the case for Curriculum Compacting. Follow the steps and move forward at your own pace and comfort level.

Classroom Scenario

Ms. Jade is a third-grade teacher who understands that instruction must be differentiated if students are to have the opportunity to flourish. She attended several conferences during the summer and read books on Differentiated Instruction. Her personal goal for the upcoming school year is to differentiate instruction in each math unit. Her ultimate goal for her students is for them to improve their standardized test scores and overall academic performance.

As is often the case, Ms. Jade's 21 students are on varying levels of readiness in regard to math skills. Several have mastered all or most of the basic concepts in previous grades and are prepared to move forward with more challenging skills. In the past, Ms. Jade would have required that all of her students complete the same assignment at the same time. She had always assumed that by doing this she was providing those who had already achieved mastery a chance to become more proficient through repeated practice. This practice allowed her to provide more assistance to her struggling students. The more advanced students felt a sense of pride in the help they provided their peers, and all of the students enjoyed the process.

Ms. Jade now realizes, however, that she had been doing a disservice to the more proficient students by neglecting to challenge them to perform at higher levels. She had been forcing them to wait for the others to catch up instead of affording them the opportunity to move forward in the curriculum.

In the upcoming unit, Ms. Jade wants to implement Curriculum Compacting to assist with expediting the learning process for basic skills in math. This process will challenge her exceptional students by pushing them to higher academic levels while allowing her weaker students to progress at their own pace.

The Differentiated Way

Planning

In previous years, Ms. Jade struggled with teaching students how to tell time. Typically, each year some students had been quite proficient while others had experienced difficulties in grasping the concept. Because of this, Ms. Jade decides that this year she will give all of her students a pretest. She carefully designs the pretest to reflect all of the different variations of time that students are expected to master in the third grade. Her test includes:

Part I   4 questions regarding time in hours
Part II   4 questions regarding time in quarter hours
Part III   4 questions regarding time in five-minute intervals
Part IV   4 questions regarding time in minutes

Ms. Jade's goal is to determine students' readiness levels so as to teach the skill in a manner that will allow for progression, continuous learning, and success for all.

She gives the students the pretest on the Friday prior to beginning the unit on telling time. This allows time for the pretest to be graded so that each student's readiness level can be determined. Students must score 3 out of 4 or higher to master each unit of time. Ms. Jade places each student's pretest scores and readiness level on a chart for quick access. Following is a sample from her class of 21 students. (Only 7 are shown here.)

Student's Name	Part 1 Hours	Part 2 Quarter Hours	Part 3 5 Minute Intervals	Part 4 Minutes	Readiness Level
Angel	3/4	2/4	1/4	0/4	III
Bailee	4/4	4/4	4/4	3/4	I
Brock	4/4	4/4	3/4	2/4	II
Gavin	4/4	3/4	3/4	3/4	I
Madison	4/4	4/4	3/4	3/4	I
Matthew	4/4	4/4	3/4	2/4	II
Nikki	3/4	2/4	0/4	0/4	III

Level I is comprised of students who have already mastered *telling time in minutes* (the current unit). These students will begin their unit of study by progressing to the more difficult skill of finding *elapsed time involving hours and minutes*. After the students master the skill, they will apply it by deciphering and solving word problems.

Level II is comprised of students who mastered the skill of *telling time in five-minute intervals*. Therefore, they are ready to progress to the more difficult skill of *telling time in minutes*. After mastery has occurred, they will progress to *finding elapsed time involving hours*.

Level III is comprised of students who have not yet mastered *telling time in quarter hours*. They will begin with quarter hours and progress toward *telling time in minutes*.

Ms. Jade determines that she will need to create three distinct lessons if she is to meet the needs of all of her students (see figure 4.13, p. 102). Her plan is to:

- compact the curriculum for the advanced students (Level I) to ensure that they receive *a more enriched area of study*. Since they have already mastered the current curriculum, they will move toward the more advanced curriculum.

- expedite the curriculum for the Level II students because they already have some prior knowledge and will be able to master the current content in a fraction of the time. (This is another level of compacting where the students are learning the *current curriculum* but are moving through it more quickly.)

- begin with the basics that have not yet been mastered for the challenged (Level III) students and provide a *slow intense curriculum* to guarantee their success and progression in the lesson.

Ms. Jade must create three separate lessons, all of which can occur simultaneously.

1. She creates a review sheet that deals with skills previously taught.

2. She creates three distinct mini lessons, which she will conduct with each group at a round table. The lessons include hands-on instruction.

3. She creates hands-on independent-practice activities, which students will complete at their desks.

4. She also creates computer-generated presentations and practice activities to be used during the process. These are constructed so as to be interactive; thus, they are captivating and motivating.

Implementation

On Monday, Ms. Jade assigns a number to each student (1, 2, or 3), which corresponds with the readiness Levels I, II, and III. She begins her unit on *telling time* by giving instructions to all:

Level I Students: *"Come to the round table and be seated."*

NOTE: These students will begin with a mini lesson. This will be followed by independent practice at their desks followed by a computer-generated game.

Level II Students: *"I am giving to you your math-review sheet. Begin working on that until I call you all to come to the round table."*

NOTE: After completing their math review sheet, students will be given a mini lesson at the round table followed by a hands-on, independent-practice activity to be completed at their desks.

Level III Students: *"I am giving to you your math-review sheet. Begin working on that. Once you have finished, move to the computers where you will view a presentation and practice telling time (in hours and half-hours). I will call you to the round table from the computers."*

NOTE: They will complete their math-review sheet first, followed by a computer generated presentation and practice activity. They will be the third group called to the round table.

Round Table Instruction

Level I Students: Ms. Jade hands each student a clock along with a sheet of paper and a pencil. She introduces the lesson and models the process for determining elapsed time. After students practice the skill and Ms. Jade is certain that all have grasped the concept, she gives each a bag containing a hands-on game (with directions) dealing with elapsed time. She explains the process involved in the game before sending them back to their desks. (She does this so as to avoid having questions arise while she is working with the next group at the round table.) She instructs them that they are to return to their desks to complete this independent practice. Once the assignment is completed, the students go to the computers to complete a special computer game, which deals with this more advanced concept: Elapsed Time.

Level II Students: She hands each student a clock and introduces her lesson: telling time to the nearest minute. Students are allowed to practice showing the time on the clock and writing the time on a sheet of paper. Ms. Jade gives them an additional hands-on assignment (which she explains in detail) and instructs them to work with these when they return to their desks.

Level III Students: Ms. Jade reviews the basic concepts of the clock from the computer presentation that they have just watched. She proceeds with the lesson on telling time in hours and half-hours and slowly progresses toward telling time in quarter hours. Students are able to practice on their individual clocks. The students then complete independent practice at the round table as Ms. Jade monitors their progress. She then has them progress to telling time in five-minute intervals. She models the skill and conducts guided instruction with them. She instructs them to return to their desks at the end of the mini lesson, and she closes the lesson with the class as a whole group.

Variations

1. Some classrooms may require more groups; some may require fewer. It depends on the readiness levels of the students.

2. Giving a pretest to all students may not be necessary. Instead, the teacher might select a few students who consistently demonstrate high achievement and give the pretest to those. She could compact the curriculum for those who show mastery on the pretest. This would

allow for whole-group instruction with the exception of only those few students who have already demonstrated mastery.

The Bottom Line

Boredom is the root of many classroom problems. When students are not being challenged, they become disinterested in the subject matter and withdraw from the lesson. Often, they wind up disturbing others. There is no need to reteach a skill that students have previously mastered. Compacting the curriculum adds vigor, which challenges students while providing them the opportunity to learn new exciting skills.

Figure 4.13
Curriculum Compacting Continuum

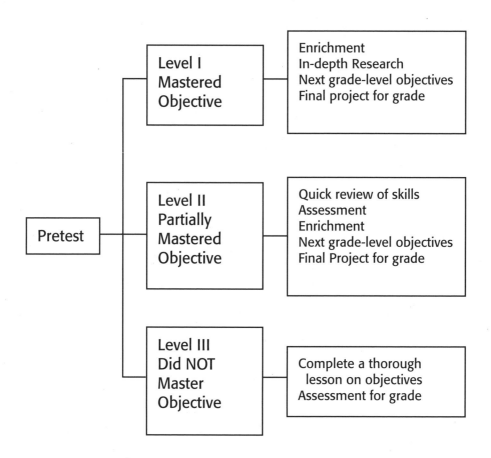

7
Anchoring Activities

I'm not opposed to learning; in fact that's why I'm here
I've listened and I've questioned, yet the reason's still unclear

If this is how it's done, and that is how it's made
Then how am I to use it when in front of me it's laid?

I wrote down every figure, every fact, and every line
I even had my parents call it out a thousand times

I used an acronym to memorize it for the test
Then on the test I set it in its final place to rest

I'm sure that there's a reason why my teacher made me learn it
I'd try to clarify it if I only could discern it

It came and went so quickly that so little I recall
Even though just days ago I thought I knew it all

One day when I am in a bind, and need to make a move
Will I know how to use it since the learning was removed?

—*Elizabeth Breaux*
from *How the BEST TEACHERS Avoid*
the 20 Most Common Teaching Mistakes

What Are They?

Challenge: *What must we teachers do to accommodate the early finishers?* It is inevitable that the time it takes for students to complete assignments will vary, and the idle time that is created as a result is often an invitation for disaster. In our attempts to prevent the early finishers from disturbing others, we often assign "busy work," which usually comes in the form of various mindless tasks that serve no purpose other than to keep the child occupied and out of trouble! Because students often perceive the "busy work" as having little or no relevance, off-task behaviors often arise. In an attempt to squelch these behaviors, teachers too often feel compelled to move ahead to the next segment of the lesson. In doing so, those students who are not yet ready are repeatedly left behind.

Learning should never cease in a classroom; its pursuit should be ongoing. Anchoring Activities are replacements for traditional "busy work." They provide early finishers the opportunity to continue their learning, thereby deepening their knowledge of the skill or topic. Anchoring Activities are meaningful, well-planned strategies that affix (anchor) students' focus on a particular concept or skill being taught, as opposed to mindless tasks created simply to keep students quiet or busy.

Anchoring Activities should be assigned after the teacher has taught the skill and built a strong, solid foundation or knowledge base. The activity should enhance the lesson and provide students the opportunity to continue learning after completing the "regular" assignment. Anchoring Activities have clearly defined expectations, purposes, and criteria for evaluating students' products, which serve to hold students accountable for their time and learning. Because they are more non-traditional in nature, these activities/ projects are most beneficial when accompanied by a rubric, which should be given to the students at the start of the activity.

When thoughtfully created, Anchoring Activities can be extremely advantageous, because they minimize off-task behaviors. They provide students with an efficient and effective use of instructional time by allowing for growth beyond the realm of the classroom discussion and activities. Because Anchoring Activities keep the early finishers moving forward, the teacher is provided the necessary time to work with individual students or small groups as needed.

When creating Anchoring Activities, make certain that they adhere to the following criteria:

- They must be meaningful and have purpose.

- They must include clear and concise directions.
- They must be built on previously learned skills.
- They must be self-directed, allowing learners to assume responsibility for their own learning.
- They must be choice-based.
- They must be differentiated to meet individual learners' needs.
- They must encourage higher-order thinking.
- They must promote individual creativity.
- They must be graded!

Following is a list of a few activities/projects that could be used as Anchoring Activities, provided that they are extensions of the current lesson or skill being taught:

- Create a book.
- Compose a skit or a song.
- Write a poem.
- Complete an experiment.
- Make a journal entry.
- Rotate through learning Centers.
- Create a Venn diagram.
- Write a news article.
- Research a topic.
- Create a model, mural, collage, or diorama.
- Play a game.
- Use technology.

Classroom Scenario

Mr. Louis is a seventh-grade life science teacher. He has 25 students of mixed ability in his class. They range from below average to more advanced. On a typical day, the "Speedy Sallys" seem to finish the given assignment before some of the "Slow Stevens" have a chance to begin. The "Speedy Sallys" invariably present the same question to Mr. Louis: "I'm finished. What do I do now?" Lately, Mr. Louis has been attempting to buy more time to work with the "Slow Stevens" by simply telling the "Speedy Sallys" to "read a book!"

Some of the "Speedy Sallys" follow his directive, while some pretend to read and others find more interesting endeavors in which to partake. The concern is that none are participating in an activity that could reinforce or deepen the knowledge base of the current skill being studied. None are participating in an activity that will allow them to connect the current lesson to prior knowledge. None are being encouraged to predict how the current lesson might influence future lessons. And none are being held accountable for the silent reading!

The Differentiated Way

Planning

Mr. Louis begins by writing all of his objectives for the unit. Then he proceeds to find activities that align with the objectives. He carefully considers the dynamics of his classroom and his students' varying abilities. After creating the initial class activities, he considers additional activity options for his early finishers. He wants desperately to create activities that will serve as meaningful extensions of the current skill being taught.

Mr. Louis collaborates with Mrs. Golden, the seventh-grade language arts teacher, for assistance. Mrs. Golden explains to Mr. Louis that the students have just finished a unit on poetry and that many of them are currently quite motivated to write poems on just about any topic! "What about having your students write poems on the various organs of the body?" she asks. Mr. Louis loves the idea. Not only could this be a wonderful Anchoring Activity for his science lesson, but it would be reinforcement of a skill being taught in another discipline. "This is cross-curricular teaching at its finest!" he thinks. Mrs. Golden helps Mr. Louis write a sample poem for each organ and build a display wall in his room for the students' final products.

Mr. Louis generates student directions packets for the Anchoring Activity (see figure 4.14, p. 109). These will ensure that early finishers can simply pick up the packets and begin the Anchoring Activity without being a disruption to those slower students who might still be working.

Implementation

Mr. Louis begins the lesson by reading the following poem to his class:

Pulsating Continuously

My heart
Is a delicate organ
Yet is strong and powerful.

My heart
Is comprised of four parts
Yet it functions as one.

My heart
Collects deoxygenated blood in the right atrium
Then ejects it through the right ventricle.

My heart
Waits for the lungs to give oxygen to the blood
Yet is patient in the process.

My heart
Collects the oxygenated blood from the lungs through the left atrium
Then ejects it to the body through the left ventricle.

My heart
Is constantly pumping
Yet it never grows tired.

After completing the poem, Mr. Louis continues. "Yesterday, we discussed the heart. This poem describes its functions and parts. Today, we will move on to the kidneys. After you have finished your assignment for the day, I want you to write a poem about the kidneys. Mrs. Golden tells me that you are great poets. I cannot wait to see your poems. You may write any type of poem that you wish." Mr. Louis places his poem on the bulletin board display and tells his students he will add their poems as they are completed. Mr. Louis points to the directions packets and says, "As soon as you have finished today's assignment, please pick up a directions packet. Within the packet you will find everything that you need to write your poem."

Mr. Louis begins his lesson. As the "Speedy Sallys" finish their assignment, they obtain the poetry directions packet (see figure 4.14, p. 109), which includes a rubric (see figure 4.15, p. 110) and begin the Anchoring Activity.

Variations

Research more in-depth information in relation to a particular organ and its functions.

1. Create a Venn Diagram comparing two organs.
2. Create a book of organs where descriptions and functions of each are included. References would be required to ensure that students include detailed information in addition to that already learned.
3. Anchoring Activities can be tiered (see Chapter 4, #4) to accommodate different levels of readiness.

The Bottom Line

To create an effective and efficient classroom environment that maximizes instructional time and promotes continuous learning, Anchoring Activities are the consummate answer to the proverbial question: *What do we do with the early finishers?*

Figure 4.14
Organ Poetry

Directions: Write a poem about the organ of the day. Include the following in your poem:

1. an appropriate/creative title for the poem

2. functions of the organ

3. purposes of the organ

NOTE: Be sure to check your completed poem for correct grammar and spelling!

Attached you will find three pages:

1. a brainstorming page

2. a rough draft page for prewriting and editing

3. a final draft page

Be creative in writing your poems. You may use the computers or additional resources in the classroom.

Figure 4.15
Organ Poetry Rubric

Title	No title 0 pts.	Inappropriate title 1 pt.	Appropriate title of poem 2 pts.	Appropriate/ Creative Title 3 pts.
Functions of organ	Not included/ inaccurate 0 pts.	One function 1 pt.	Two functions included 2 pts.	Three functions included 3pts.
Purpose of organ	Not included/ inaccurate 0 pts.	Weak explanation 1 pt.	Explanation with little detail 2 pts.	Detailed explanation 3 pts.
Grammar/ Spelling	More than 9 mistakes 0 pts.	5–8 mistakes 1 pt.	1–4 mistakes 2 pts.	0 mistakes 3pts.

8
Varying Questioning

My teacher makes me think too much
He asks too many questions
Not the easy "yes" or "no" kind
His require expression.

And even if I answer right
He doesn't stop it there
He makes me answer "Why" or "How"
"What if?" "What then?" (Who cares?).

He calls this "higher order thinking"
(I'll tell him what I think...
On second thought, if I did that
My grades would surely sink.)

So I'll just play the game with him
I know it makes him happy
(But all this thinking makes me tired
I think I'll take a "nappy.")

—Elizabeth Breaux
from *Classroom Management SIMPLIFIED*

What Is It?

When devising pertinent questions to ask students during a given lesson, we must first explore why we formulate and ask questions of our learners and the importance of the timing of specific questions during the lesson cycle. There are three crucial points in a lesson where questioning students is imperative. At each of these points, the teacher should pose questions that prepare the learner for success at the next point. The three crucial points and reasons for questioning at those points are as follows:

Beginning of the lesson cycle:
- access prior knowledge
- encourage predictions
- determine readiness level of students
- build suspense
- relate the topic to previous information or lessons
- give students a direction for the lesson

During the lesson:
- break from the lecture
- assess understanding/informal assessment
- promote discussion and retention
- keep students on task and manage behavior
- determine that ideas and concepts are understood

End of the lesson:
- determine if information was retained (informal assessment)
- provide closure
- connect the lesson to past or future lessons

The impact that the beginning of any lesson has on students is central to the rest of the lesson, because it is at that point that we either hook our learners and encourage engagement, or lose them altogether. An engaging introduction should be creatively designed. Questions should include those that help the learners to connect prior knowledge to today's lesson. Students should be encouraged to make predictions and share questions that they would like to have answered by the end of the lesson. When introducing a new concept, give students leading questions that will help guide them through the lesson.

It is imperative that pertinent questions continue to be asked throughout the lesson and then again at its closure.

The questions must be varied to accommodate for the many *levels of readiness* and *levels of thinking* that exist within the walls of one classroom.

- **Level of Readiness** is the point at which a student is functioning in relation to his/her understanding of a specific concept.

  NOTE: It is easy to underestimate a student's readiness level. For instance, Joe's reading level is two grade levels lower than his current placement. It is usually difficult for Joe to gain a firm understanding of new topics because his attention span is so short. The teacher introduces the human body and discovers that Joe is fascinated with the human body. He watches *Discovery Health* on television most weekends and regularly checks out books on the human body. He can name all of the parts and functions of the body. Joe's readiness level for the human body is high. He is a prime example of how readiness levels can change for students depending on their interest and exposure to a specific topic. Joe's reading level is generally lower than is expected at his current grade level, but in this case, he will be able to read material dealing with the body at a higher level because he has acquired prior knowledge of it. This exposure has afforded him a repertoire of words in his vocabulary that relate to the concept.

- **Level of Thinking** refers to the type of questions that students are asked to answer. Questions must be leveled and on a broad spectrum from basic recalling of information on up to complex evaluating of subject matter. Students will not develop the ability to think critically if they are not challenged on a daily basis. To assist with leveled questions, use Bloom's hierarchy of thinking.

Benjamin Bloom's Taxonomy of Cognitive Development

Knowledge—remembering information
Comprehension—knowing the meaning of the information
Application—using the information
Analysis—breaking the information down into smaller pieces
Synthesis—putting the pieces into a new whole
Evaluation—formulating judgments based on the information

One suggestion for ensuring that questions are varied is to ask one higher-order question for every two lower-order questions. This is often a difficult task to accomplish because asking lower-order questions comes naturally.

Preparing all questions in advance will guarantee that varied questioning occurs. This process will become easier with time and practice. (As we've all learned through experience, *time changes nothing if we don't change what we do in that time...*) The practice, however, must be deliberate and well thought-out to become second nature. The amount of time it takes for it to become natural depends on the individual teacher.

Classroom Scenario

The staff at Moore Middle School is on a mission to increase students' test scores. Teachers are being asked to challenge students by asking a wide array of questions.

The state tests require students to use critical-thinking skills. When teachers neglect to equip students with those skills on a daily basis, they will perform poorly on such tests.

Teachers have been asked to complete a personal inventory by answering the following questions:

- Do I question my students at critical points during every lesson to ascertain whether or not learning is occurring?
- Do I question students in a manner that encourages purposeful reflective and insightful thinking?
- Does variation in questioning exist in regard to levels of thinking (Bloom's Taxonomy)?
- Do lower-order (basic knowledge and recall) questions outweigh those that encourage critical thinking?

After giving these questions close consideration, most teachers agreed that they would have to answer "no" to most or all of them. This was a good starting point because, as we teachers have all learned, the impetus for change is the acknowledgement that change is necessary. Acknowledgement of a problem is always the first step toward rectifying it.

After attending two days of staff development on *Higher-Order Thinking Skills*, teachers returned to their classrooms armed with the knowledge and skills necessary to employ the proper changes. Fortunately, many of them had the will to make changes. Regrettably, some did not.

"Will" and "drive" were two words that had never been used to describe Mr. Fester. He had been teaching the same way and using the same techniques for so many years that his former students were able to share saved tests and notes from their days in his classroom with their own children! As was expected each year, his students posted some of the lowest scores in the school. Unfortunately, that too would remain unchanged.

Mr. Resolve, on the other hand, whose reputation for his determination and tenacity preceded him, resolved to seize the mission at hand. He returned home on that Friday afternoon with a plan that he intended to put into action on the following Monday. So much to do. No time to waste....

The Differentiated Way

Planning

Mr. Resolve opened his lesson plans for the following week and began to study them. A close look revealed what he already knew: planning for specific types of questions at various levels of thinking and at critical points in the lesson was something that he had not been doing. He had allowed questioning to be completely spontaneous (some of which is a good thing). In doing so, higher-order questions had seldom been asked and questioning students at critical points in the lessons had been completely overlooked.

He began perusing several tests and quizzes that he had given in the previous weeks and was equally disappointed. Careful study of individual questions revealed that most were at very basic levels, where recall of information was virtually all that had been required of students:

1. Who was the leader of the Union during the Civil War?

2. How many troops served in the Confederate Army?

3. In what year did the Civil War begin?

4. Who was the president during the Civil War?

5. What colors did opposing sides wear in the Civil War?

6. What is a bayonet?

He referred to Elizabeth Breaux's *Start Words* chart (see figure 4.16, p. 121), which had been given to all teachers at the inservice session, and began formulating questions that he would use during the lesson and some that he would use on the quiz and the test. The *Start Words* (which follow the hierarchy of Bloom's taxonomy) were a guide that helped him to devise questions using words that would determine levels of thought necessary to formulate answers. He began with the lowest level, "Knowledge," which is what he had overused in the past, and moved upward to the higher levels of "Analysis,

Synthesis, and Evaluation." He realized that in the past he had been asking many "yes/no" type questions, along with others that required so little thought that one-word answers would often suffice. By using the *Start Words* chart, the overuse of such questions would be remedied.

He began by deciding upon the content of the questions that would be used at the three crucial points (beginning, middle, and end) of the lesson, and then chose *Start Words* that would promote and develop the use of critical-thinking skills in his students.

Beginning:

1. Does anyone know the meaning of the word "civil?"

2. Now that we know the meaning of the word "civil," what is your interpretation of a civil war?

3. How might civil wars begin?

4. Would it be possible for soldiers on opposing sides of a civil war to know one another personally? How might that affect a battle?

5. Can anyone tell us what you already know about the Civil War that began in our country in 1861? What more might you like to know about the Civil War?

6. Considering the era in which the Civil War occurred, what types of weapons do you think might have been used?

7. What might have been some repercussions of the use of such weapons?

8. What types of weapons used today were not in existence during the Civil War?

9. Has anyone ever seen a movie based on the events of the Civil War? Would you like to share what you remember from the movie?

During:

1. In what ways were soldiers who fought for opposing sides during the Civil War alike? How did they differ?

2. Why, do you think, some family members actually chose opposing sides during the Civil War?

3. Describe your feelings concerning the fact that many slaves actually fought for the South during the Civil War.

4. How might a civil war in one country affect another country?

5. Design a newspaper headline for the Civil War of 2035.

6. Give your own explanation for why slavery was so widely accepted by some, and so vehemently opposed by others.

After:

1. Identify Abraham Lincoln's strengths as a leader. How might the events of the Civil War have been different had he not possessed such strengths?

2. The Civil War was fought for several reasons. What might have happened to this country had the war not been fought?

3. What do you predict might be reasons for future civil wars that were not issues in past ones?

4. We know that slavery was abolished as a result of the Civil War. In your opinion, however, were slaves really freed?

Knowing that some of these questions might be difficult, at first, for students to comprehend, Mr. Resolve planned to take as much time as necessary to assist them in deciphering the questions. He realized that it was his own fault that many of his students were unable to decipher and answer higher-order questions. How could they when they had not been challenged to do so?

Mr. Fester, on the other hand, had no intention of challenging his students at higher levels. His reason was that the students would not be able to answer such higher-order questions, so why bother?

Mr. Resolve knew that if he did nothing, there would be no chance of their developing the skills. His expectations were high, but he knew better than to expect too much too soon. It would take a while for students to adjust to these higher-order questions. He decided that he would include in his plan the names of particular students who would be called on to answer specific questions. This would accomplish two things:

1. It would guarantee that all students would become active participants in the lesson.

2. It would ensure that individual readiness levels were accounted for when questions were assigned.

Implementation

NOTE: Years of experience as a teacher of history have taught Mr. Resolve that students will engage in a lesson regarding a particular period in history when they can relate it to something familiar. He planned to do just that before introducing them to the events of the Civil War.

Mr. Resolve began his lesson by telling a story about two men, brothers, who became members of opposing gangs in New York City, and how they found themselves face to face on opposing sides of a gang fight. Afterwards, he allowed students to give their opinions as to what might have happened to cause this and how it might have been avoided.

Afterwards, he began asking the questions that he had prepared for the beginning of the lesson. A visual representation of the questions was included to assist those who would need to see as well as to hear the questions. As he had expected, it was necessary for him to help some of the students decipher certain questions, because they were not accustomed to the higher-order format. The fact that the questions were visually displayed assisted in this.

The entire lesson on the Civil War lasted about a week, which gave Mr. Resolve several opportunities to assess progress at key points throughout the lesson. The questions in the previous section were used along with others that he created along the way. Written mini assessments were given several times during the week in the form of two-to-three question "spot checks," as Mr. Resolve referred to them. Initially, he assisted students with the question translation because many were unfamiliar with it, but as the lesson progressed, he began to notice that the students were becoming more familiar with the higher-order questions. Their abilities to think in more critical terms were escalating. The small daily successes led to greater ones. Students were more engaged in the lessons, and achievement was rising. They were very capable! It was he who had not been giving them the chance!

In the meantime, Mr. Fester's students were napping as Mr. Fester lectured….

Variations

Varying the types of questions during the lesson used can be achieved through an array of methods, but regardless of which methods are used, questions must be asked at the three crucial points throughout the lesson.

Following is a particular variation that we have enjoyed using with our own students. We call it *Big Questions.*

- Prepare several boxes of questions, enough boxes for several groups of students. Make sure that each question is written on its own slip of paper. (Answers to the questions should be prepared in advance and written on a separate sheet of paper.)

- Question types should vary so that they address all levels of thinking. On the back of each question slip, write the number of points that will be awarded for a correct answer.

> Knowledge = 1 point
>
> Comprehension = 2 points
>
> Application = 3 points
>
> Analysis = 4 points
>
> Synthesis = 5 points
>
> Evaluation = 6 points

- Place students in groups of three or four. One student must be the designated scorekeeper for each group while the others play the game. Students can take turns serving as the scorekeeper so that all students are able to participate in the game.
- Whole groups can compete against one another, or individual students within each group can compete against one another.
- Question slips are then drawn from the boxes. If the correct answer is given by the student who draws the slip, the scorekeeper (who possesses the answer sheet) awards the correct amount of points. If individuals are playing against one another, incorrectly answered questions would be placed into the box to be drawn by another group member. If groups are competing against groups where all group members are working together to determine a correct answer, place the question off to the side if it cannot be correctly answered by the group as a whole.
- The teacher should closely monitor this activity so that informal assessing can occur.

The Bottom Line

When preparing a lesson we must:

1. Prepare questions that are appropriate for use at the three crucial points in any lesson:
   a. beginning
   b. during
   c. end

2. Make certain that questions take into account the array of *readiness levels* that exists within one group of students. Specific questions should be prepared for specific students.

3. Ensure that questions address the various *levels of thinking* (according to Bloom's Taxonomy) so that students are encouraged to think critically.

Students must be trained to think critically. A brain that is not challenged will not grow. We cannot expect students to perform at higher levels if they have not become accustomed to doing so on a daily basis.

Do not allow the destructive philosophies of the "Mr. Festers" to permeate your school. Students can learn, but only if the teachers meet them at their readiness levels and encourage success at those levels before moving them forward. The ability to think critically is a life skill. Let's prepare our students for life!

Figure 4.16
Start Words

Knowledge	Comprehension	Applications	Analysis	Synthesis	Evaluation
Name	Predict	Apply	Analyze	Rearrange	Recommend
List	Discuss	Demonstrate	Separate	Design	Support
Define	Estimate	Classify	Infer	Compose	Judge
Label	Summarize	Relate	Compare	Plan	Convince
Describe	Interpret	Solve	Arrange	What if?	Conclude
Who?	Describe	Change	Explain	Rewrite	Discriminate
What?	Distinguish	Examine	Connect	Invent	Rank

LOWER LEVEL ----► ----► ----► ----► **HIGHER LEVEL**

Created by Elizabeth Breaux using research from Bloom's Taxonomy

9
Connect Four

If given the choice of a "can" or a "can't"
As opposed to a "will" or a "won't"
A "can't" is as good as a "can" if he will
Where a "can" is no use if he won't!

A "can't" with the will can attain what a "won't"
Can't attain even though that he can
For a "will" is much stronger and always lasts longer
Than he who will not understand.

A "won't" never will, but a "can't" can learn still
In spite of at present cannot
If he simply believes in his will to achieve
There is nothing he ever will not!

—Elizabeth Breaux

What Is It?

Connect Four is a creative strategy for affording students flexibility in learning while allowing their competitive sides to be challenged. Connect Four is an excellent way to excite students after introducing a skill or concept. It may also be used to prepare or review for a test. Furthermore, it is designed so that students are encouraged to think critically, at varying levels of difficulty, as was just discussed in the previous section, #8 *Varying Questioning.*

In Connect Four, students are given a worksheet (which resembles a board game) consisting of 16 squares (see figure 4.17, p. 124). Each square on the board contains one question. To complete the game, students must correctly answer four questions that are connected to one another vertically, horizontally, or diagonally. Because the Connect Four board consists of a total of 16 questions/squares, 10 possible Connect Four options exist.

The 16 questions should be written so as to encourage critical thought at various levels of Bloom's Taxonomy. This will ensure that students are hardpressed to develop and perfect higher-order thinking skills that require individual creative thought (and answers). The *Start Words* chart (see figure 4.16, p. 121 from the previous section) will help in the development of the questions. Four connected questions on a Connect Four board could be leveled according to levels of difficulty as follows:

1. **low**—Requires basic *Knowledge* and *Comprehension* skills.

2. **medium**—Requires *Application* skills.

3. **high**—Encourages *Analytical* thinking.

4. **challenging**—Encourages ability to *Synthesize* and come to *Evaluative* conclusions.

The teacher should construct predetermined acceptable answers for each question. Detail in answering questions should be encouraged.

Connect Four can be played in a non-competitive way either individually or with a partner. In a non-competitive version of the activity, students might simply be awarded points for any four correctly answered questions. The game can also be played competitively where two players are forced to think strategically in order to correctly answer specific questions that are connected while attempting to block their opponent from doing the same. The first to connect four correctly answered questions wins.

Using a format such as the one that follows in figure 4.17 will ensure that all levels of questioning are intermixed. The numbers represent the various levels of questioning, from Low to Challenging.

Figure 4.17
Connect Four

2 Medium	1	4	3
4	3 High	2	1
3	4	1 Low	2
1	2	3	4 Challenging

When creating your Connect Four boards, be sure that ample space is given for answers, because students will write answers directly on the board. (Another option is to allow students to write answers on a separate sheet of paper.) Formulating questions for your Connect Four board may be a little difficult at first. We have included a model (see figure 4.18, p. 125) of a board that uses *Start Words* (see figure 4.16, p. 121) to ensure that questions are written on various levels of questioning (low, medium, high, challenging).

Figure 4.18
Connect Four

Describe.... Answer:_____ _____ _____ _____	Label.... Answer:_____ _____ _____ _____	Predict.... Answer:_____ _____ _____ _____	Illustrate.... Answer:_____ _____ _____ _____
Argue... Answer:_____ _____ _____ _____	Discuss... Answer:_____ _____ _____ _____	Solve... Answer:_____ _____ _____ _____	Name... Answer:_____ _____ _____ _____
Demonstrate... Answer:_____ _____ _____ _____	Create... Answer:_____ _____ _____ _____	List... Answer:_____ _____ _____ _____	Explain... Answer:_____ _____ _____ _____
Define... Answer:_____ _____ _____ _____	Identify... Answer:_____ _____ _____ _____	Write... Answer:_____ _____ _____ _____	Compare/ Contrast... Answer:_____ _____ _____ _____

Connect Four meets the needs of all students by permitting flexibility in the formatting of the game. Samantha Slow, who is reading below level and has difficulty completing assigned tasks in timely fashion, might be given a board that includes a "free" space or a board that includes more lower than higher-level questions. The free space would allow Samantha to spend additional time on her other questions, which in this case might be the better option. Chad Challenge might be given a board that includes more higher than lower-level questions.

Classroom Scenario

Mrs. Kim is an elementary teacher faced with the challenge that many of us have encountered throughout our years of teaching: teaching identical subject matter to a diverse group of students. Her class consists of 25 students who range from *extremely challenged* to *gifted* in reading ability. Teaching the class as a whole group has proven to be ineffective.

Mrs. Kim has become more conscious of the fact that the old saying, "Necessity is the father of invention," is more pertinent in her classroom this year than it has ever been. She must devise creative strategies that will promote learning for all students, regardless of readiness, ability, and thinking levels. She must invent new strategies for reaching and teaching all of her students. Those strategies will ensure success for all and boredom for none.

Her class is about to begin reading one of the required novels for the grade level. She must devise a way to assist the struggling readers without impeding the progress of those who are more advanced in reading ability.

She has used "Connect Four" in past years as a hands-on review activity that assisted students in preparing for an assessment or in reinforcing skills already taught. During the reading of this novel she plans to use it primarily as an ongoing teaching/assessing tool. She will divide the book into several sections. As students complete each section they will be required to complete the Connect Four activity that accompanies that section before moving on to the next section.

The Differentiated Way

Planning

Mrs. Kim divides the novel into five separate sections comprised of 2–3 chapters each.

1. section I   chapters 1–3
2. section II   chapters 4–6
3. section III   chapters 7–8
4. section IV   chapters 9–11
5. section V   chapters 12–13

She divides her students into three categories based on reading levels:

- low (struggling)
- average
- above average

Because the class consists of these three fairly distinct categories, three different Connect Four boards are created to accompany each section of the novel.

Next, she prepares the logistics:

1. Students will work individually on this particular novel, but they will be placed into three categories, each category represented by a color. Students will be oblivious to the real reason for the distinction in color. They will simply believe that it means that three different sets of Connect Four boards with different questions will be circulating the room. (This ensures that distinctions between various learning levels are not obvious.)

   - Green = low
   - Yellow = average
   - Red = above average

2. Mrs. Kim will create colored note cards (green, yellow, and red), which will be placed on the students' desks to identify the category in which they are performing.

3. The Connect Four boards will be created with these three distinct colors. (The *Start Words* chart on p. 121 can assist in formulating questions for the three different-colored boards.)

   - The **green (low) boards** will consist of questions taken primarily from the low to medium range of Bloom's Taxonomy.

   - The **yellow (average) boards** will consist of questions taken primarily from the medium range of Bloom's Taxonomy, with some from both the lower and higher ends of the range.

   - The **red (above average) boards** will contain questions taken primarily from the mid and upper ranges of Bloom's Taxonomy.

4. For this particular novel, Mrs. Kim will require students to complete two Connect Four options per game board before another section of the novel is read. (At times she may choose to have students complete

the entire board of questions before proceeding to the next section of the novel.)

5. Mrs. Kim's role will be to monitor, assist, correct questions, and assess students' progress.

   NOTE: As levels of thinking increase, Mrs. Kim may choose to move students to a higher category (different color) for upcoming sections of the novel.

Implementation

NOTE: Mrs. Kim places the colored cards on the students' desks before students arrive. The three categories (low, average, above average) have been predetermined to save time.

Students enter the room and notice the cards on their desks. Mrs. Kim begins explaining the procedure to the students. Because this is the first time the Connect Four activity has been used with this group, an explanation is necessary before students begin reading the novel.

- She distributes the Connect Four boards and explains the procedure for the activity. Once procedural questions have been answered, she collects the boards.

- She distributes the novels and begins the introductory activities by first reading the opening paragraph and then stopping for discussion to:
  1. make connections to prior knowledge.
  2. share a personal story and allow students to share related experiences.
  3. check for current knowledge of the novel's content.
  4. ask probing questions (i.e., What would you like to know?).

- She refers to the five sections of the novel that are written on the board, explaining that upon completion of each section, a Connect Four activity will commence.

  1. Section I—Read chapters 1–3
     Connect Four activity

  2. Section II—Read chapters 4–6
     Connect Four activity

3. Section III—Read chapters 7–8
   Connect Four activity

4. Section IV—Read chapters 9–11
   Connect Four activity

5. Section V—Read chapters 12–13
   Connect Four activity

- She instructs students to begin reading.

- As students begin completing Section I, she delivers the appropriate Connect Four boards and students attempt to make two separate Connect Four connections. Mrs. Kim monitors ongoing progress of students, clarifies questions when necessary, and conducts informal assessments. Students work until two "Connect Fours" are correctly completed. Mrs. Kim checks the boards as students complete the two Connect Four connections. At that time, Mrs. Kim collects the board from the student, and the student begins reading the next section.

NOTE: This process continues for several days and as expected, the students finish reading the novel at varying times. Mrs. Kim has anticipated this and has created extremely challenging Connect Four boards for the early finishers. These serve as enrichment activities for the above-average students while affording the extra time for Mrs. Kim to spend assisting the low and average groups.

Variations

1. Allow the entire class to use one board. Include a free space.

2. Change the name of the game to reflect different strategies:

   - *Blackout*: Students must complete an entire board of questions.
   - *Any Eight, Any Ten*: Students answer a given number of questions from anywhere on the board.

3. Make it competitive:

   - Create groups who will work together to complete a board. Groups might compete against one another.
   - Allow competition between individual students.

The Bottom Line

When allowed to use a hands-on, game-like approach to learning, students automatically engage in the process. Off-task behaviors are rare, and when they do occur they are more easily rectified. The Connect Four approach is fun, learning-oriented, and easily implemented, while providing the differentiation needed to meet various needs of learners. The hard work comes in the planning phase, but the benefits are worth the effort!

10
RAFT

I'm bound and determined, persistent and driven
I'll run with the ball, but not 'til it's given
I'll persevere through the toughest of times
But not without impetus, reason, or rhyme.

Hand the baton and I'll be on my way
I'll run through the tape or I simply won't play
Given the tools and afforded the chance
I'll sing any song…..I'll dance any dance.

—*Elizabeth Breaux*

What Is It?

All too often, we teachers require that students write essays to demonstrate their knowledge of subject matter. Then, we frequently endure countless hours of reading and correcting the same mundane, thoughtless essays. Because the essays are not well thought-out by the writer, they are not thought-provoking to the reader. Therefore, they are boring and difficult to score!

RAFT is a writing activity used to demonstrate the understanding of informational text in a non-traditional way. RAFT activities give the students the structure and flexibility necessary for them to become more creative with their writing, by assigning specifics with which the writer is to work. Each letter of the acronym, RAFT, symbolizes a specific component of the writing piece:

R—Role of the writer—Who you are? (reporter, doctor, teacher, etc.)

A—Audience for the writing—Who is the reader? (employer, teacher, etc.)

F—Format of the writing—What type of writing will be utilized? (article, letter, etc.)

T—Topic—What is the subject? (reasons for the war, health care, author's point of view, etc.)

In the real world, we automatically plan our writing with consideration to role, audience, format, and topic. For example, a person in search of a job writes a letter to the human resources manager of the company. He/she instinctively knows to use the following plan:

R—Role: someone looking for a job with this company

A—Audience: Human Resources Manager of the company

F—Format: letter with resume

T—Topic: his/her interest in the job and compelling reasons he/she should be hired

Consider another real-life example: A politician prepares to speak to a large group in an effort to rally their support. He/she automatically uses the RAFT format:

R—He/she takes the *Role* of "Best Candidate for the Job."

A—He/she writes with the *Audience,* potential supporters who have certain needs, interests, concerns, etc., in mind.

F—He/she knows that a speech is the most appropriate *Format*.

T—He/she knows that, if he is to garner audience support, his *Topic* must be geared toward what they need and what they want to hear.

RAFT writing inspires creativity and critical thought. It forces students to process information learned and to elaborate on it instead of regurgitating it in typical essay format. In lieu of the conventional essay assignment, give students a RAFT chart and allow them to choose the *Role, Audience, Format, and Topic*. Another option would be for the teacher to assign all components of the RAFT. A third option might be to assign only one or two components of the RAFT and then allow for choice in the remaining categories. Following is a sample RAFT chart. (Components have not been assigned.)

Role	Audience	Format	Topic

Following are the steps for creating and completing a RAFT chart:

1. Using current or previous subject matter, create *Topic* options.

2. Develop a variety of *Roles* that students could assume in their writing.

3. Brainstorm (with students) a selection of *Audiences* that might be interested in various topics.

4. Determine types of writing *Formats* of which students have knowledge.

Suggestion: Think of strong verbs that will add vigor to the students' writings. The strong verbs are used to persuade an audience and/or to analyze a situation. If using the strong verbs, add an "S" to the acronym (so that it becomes RAFTS) and an "S" column to the chart.

The teacher may choose to create a generic chart that holds numerous options. The "Topic" column might be left blank and filled in to accommodate changing subject matter (see figure 4.19, p. 141). The activity might begin with student selections of topics.

- The students may want to brainstorm some facts about specific *topics (T)* to ensure that they have enough information.

- Next, each student selects a *role (R)* in which he/she will be writing. The role (or voice) is important because the student will become that character or object.

- After selecting a role, the student must choose an *audience (A)* to whom the role would appeal. The student is now charged with the responsibility of determining what is important to the audience. What does the audience want to know? How does the audience feel about a topic? What and why is this topic important to this audience? How can the writer appeal to them emotionally?

- Finally, the student must determine the most appropriate *format (F)* to convey the information to the audience.

This process allows students to make decisions about their own writing. It allows students to be creative and have fun with writing while demonstrating their depth of understanding and knowledge of the topic. It gives students choice in the format of the product they are creating. The students' writings are authentic and written for a purpose. Students are challenged to consider the audience's perspective. This inspires students to think deeply and critically about the topic and to communicate their knowledge and their feelings through their writing.

RAFT writing can be used in any subject area. Students may be asked to write the RAFT with or without notes, books, or resources. The RAFT concept is a perfect way to differentiate instruction in that the charts can be tailored to meet the needs of individuals (more on this in the "Planning" and "Implementation" sections on pp. 135–140).

Classroom Scenario

Mr. Bradley is an eighth-grade science teacher. His students have just completed a health unit on *Obesity and the Nation-Wide Epidemic of Overweight People in the United States.* Mr. Bradley decides that he will use a RAFT writing assignment as a means of assessing students' knowledge. Because Mr. Bradley's students are on varying ability and readiness levels, he must accommodate these differences in the planning and implementation phases.

The Differentiated Way

Planning

NOTE: Mr. Bradley is not an English/language arts/writing teacher, so he elicits the help of a teacher who can assist him. Mrs. Barker helps him with the specifics and provides the necessary guidelines for the various writing formats. Mr. Bradley has been careful to include only those that Mrs. Barker has already taught to the students: article, brochure, journal entry, speech, news story, and letter.

Mr. Bradley considers several sub-topics that would fall under the broad topic, *Obesity and the Nation-Wide Epidemic of Overweight People in the United States,* and places those in the "Topic" column of his RAFT chart. He then devises some interesting roles that could be assumed by the writer. He follows that by inserting out-of-the-ordinary audiences and appropriate formats as seen in the following chart.

Role	Audience	Format	Topic
Doctor	Young children	Article	Effects of obesity on the heart
Heart	Reader	Brochure	Dangers of obesity
Hamburger	French fries	Journal Entry	Facts about obesity
Fictional character	Body part	Speech	Obesity and physical limitations
Journalist	Group of hamburgers	News story	Ways to prevent obesity
Patient	Unhealthy foods	Letter	Causes of obesity

Because this is the first time the students will use the RAFT format as a writing structure, he plans for a thorough introduction and explanation of the activity. He decides that he will assign/specify only one component, the "Format" component, and allow student choice in *Role, Audience,* and *Topic.* According to Mrs. Barker, five students in particular have been struggling with the letter-writing format. By assigning that particular format, letter writing, to these students, he will be able to accommodate their need for a tutorial, which will come in the form of the individual assistance he will be able to give to them while others are working on their own individual RAFT. He obtains a RAFT Skeleton Letter from Mrs. Barker to help assist these five students once the activity begins (see figure 4.20, p. 142).

He decides that he will present the RAFT activity to the whole class and then give students examples of how they might proceed. Following are some choices that he will present:

1. You are a doctor writing an article for a health magazine on the facts about obesity. These would be the components of your RAFT:
   R: *Doctor*
   A: *Reader*
   F: *Article*
   T: *Facts about obesity*

2. You are a hamburger writing a speech to present to a group of hamburgers warning them about the dangers of obesity. These would be the components of your RAFT:
   R: *Hamburger*
   A: *Group of hamburgers*
   F: *Speech*
   T: *Dangers of obesity*

3. You are a fictional character writing a speech to deliver to young children about over-eating and the effects of obesity on the heart. These would be the components of your RAFT:
   R: *Fictional character*
   A: *Young children*
   F: *Speech*
   T: *Effects of obesity on the heart*

Mr. Bradley obtains skeletons and/or models of all writing formats from Mrs. Barker in the event that students need reinforcement of what she has already taught. He also creates rubrics that will be presented and used to score each assignment.

Mr. Bradley plans his *"Attention Grabber"* (his name for it). He will assume the role of a heart, and will have his students assume the roles of unhealthy foods. He plans a speech that he will give before introducing the RAFT.

Implementation

NOTE: It is important to note that students have been studying the topic of *Obesity and the nation-wide epidemic of overweight people in the United States* for several days now, so today's lesson is based on previous knowledge.

The students enter the room laughing. How could they not laugh? Their teacher is standing in the hallway, his face painted red, and wearing a costume that makes him appear to be a very large, highly diseased, well-used and abused heart! He hands out cards to each student as they enter the room. On each card is written the names/descriptions of a previously agreed upon unhealthy food:

- fried chicken
- cheese fries
- potato chips
- greasy hamburger
- thick chocolate malt
- all meat and cheese pizza
- supreme dream burrito

The bell rings. The students are squealing with laughter. Mr. Bradley proceeds to move from the doorway to the front of the room, where he is standing facing his audience. He begins to speak:

"You laugh at me now, don't you? What you do not realize is that you are the reason that I am in this current condition of decay. I have not always looked this way. Years ago, when I looked into a mirror, this is what I saw." (He holds up a picture of a perfectly healthy heart for all to see.)

Pause...

"You laugh at me now, but you do not realize that I live inside all of you. This picture (again he holds up the picture of the healthy heart) is one of me long ago, inside of you now, knowing that I will not look like this for much longer. For every one of you (he walks the room pointing to the various food cards that have been handed out to the students) that enters the mouth of my human, I enter the next stage of my decay. My human is long gone, leaving only me here, alone, dead, and decayed...."

He pretends to die, slowly giving way until he is slumped over a chair. He collapses onto the floor. The students cheer!

Mr. Bradley rises and takes a bow. He displays the RAFT Chart for all to see, and begins questioning students, referring to the chart with each question:

Role	Audience	Format	Topic
Doctor	Young children	Article	Effects of obesity on the heart
Heart	Reader	Brochure	Dangers of obesity
Hamburger	French fries	Journal entry	Facts about obesity
Fictional character	Body part	Speech	Obesity and physical limitations
Journalist	Group of hamburgers	News story	Ways to prevent obesity
Patient	Unhealthy foods	Letter	Causes of obesity

1. What *role* did I just assume? (He points to the *Role* column, and students answer that he was a *heart*.)

2. Who was my *audience*? (He points to the *Audience* column, and students agree that they, the *unhealthy foods*, were his audience.)

3. What *format* did I use to deliver my message? (He points to the *Format* column, and students concur that this was a *speech*.)

4. What was the *topic* of my message? (He points to the *Topic* column, and students decide that the most appropriate topic was *Effects of obesity on the heart*.)

He proceeds with a discussion of the RAFT format for writing. He shows, through examples, how the RAFT allows for creativity in the writing and relaying of a message. He asks students if they would have preferred to have been given notes on the topic or to have had this creative speech used instead that would deliver the same message. Students all agreed that the speech was much more interesting and engaging. He refers to the RAFT chart and then presents the sample choices that he has prepared as further proof that writing using the RAFT will make their own writings much more creative and interesting:

1. You are a *doctor* writing an article for a health magazine on the facts of obesity. These would be the components of your RAFT:
   R: *Doctor*
   A: *Reader*
   F: *Article*
   T: *Facts about obesity*

2. You are a *hamburger* writing a speech to present to a group of hamburgers warning them about the dangers of obesity. These would be the components of your RAFT:

   R: *Hamburger*
   A: *Group of hamburgers*
   F: *Speech*
   T: *Dangers of obesity*

3. You are *a fictional character* writing a speech to young children about over-eating and the effects of obesity on the heart. These would be the components of your RAFT:

   R: *Fictional character*
   A: *Young children*
   F: *Speech*
   T: *Effects on the heart*

He proceeds with this first RAFT activity by assigning specific writing formats (F) to students. Before students are allowed to begin, he completes the following preliminary tasks that he has planned:

1. He holds a brief review (of the previously learned material on obesity) in the form of a discussion.

2. He reviews and gives brief examples of the various writing formats.

3. He makes available to the students the skeletons for each writing format.

4. He distributes the scoring rubrics and explains each.

Students begin working on their RAFT. Mr. Bradley is now available to spend more time working with those students who need more individualized attention. He is also able to monitor all students to ascertain that the RAFT is being completed as directed, since this is the first time that it is being used.

Mr. Bradley is especially pleased with the on-task behaviors:

- All students are engaged.
- Students are asking relevant questions.
- Students are talking, but the discussions all pertain to the activity.
- Students are eager to share their work with others.
- The motivation has spurred creativity, and students seem very proud of their original works.

- Cross-curricular teaching (See Chapter 4, *#12 Team Teaching*) is being implemented at its finest, with Mr. Bradley, the science teacher, concurring with the English teacher to reinforce writing skills within a science classroom.

Variations

- Allow students to role play when presenting the RAFT to the class.
- Instead of using the RAFT as an assessment tool, use it for remediation and/or enrichment purposes.
- Assign a specified number of strong verbs (see figure 4.19, p. 141) to be used in the RAFT and allow students complete choice in all components. This will force them to use critical-thinking skills to determine the components that would best accommodate the assigned strong verbs.

The Bottom Line

Many students hate to write… and many teachers detest grading the papers of those students! The reason is simple: the writing assignments often lack meaning, purpose, structure, and the potential for creativity. The RAFT format addresses all of these issues, while at the same time lending itself to differentiation. It can be easily implemented in classrooms across the curriculum. Because meaning, purpose, and creativity are encouraged, structure and attention to detail become more evident. This makes for better writing and easier grading, resulting in less aversion to the entire process for students and teachers. The real-life skill of writing should never be one that is loathed!

Figure 4.19

Generic RAFT(S) chart for easy use. Just fill in the topic.

Role	Audience	Format	Topic	Strong Verbs
Actor/Actress	Actor/Actress	Advertisement		align
Air	Adult	Announcement		analyze
Animal	Animal/Insect	Article		announce
Attorney	Arena of poeple	Book		apply
Body part	Artist	Brochure		brainstorm
Building	Body part	Debate		charm
Camera	Cartoon characters	Directions		clarify
Cartoon character	Children	Editorial		communicate
Citizen	Community	E-mail		compare
Clothing	Doctor	Eulogy		consider
Computer	Fictional character	Greeting Card		construct
Doctor	Friend/family	Instructions		contemplate
Food	Future owner	Interview		create
Garbage	Group member	Invitation		decipher
Girl/Boy	Health Department	Journal entry		describe
Governor	Historian	Letter/note		distinguish
Historian	Internet user	List		embellish
Insect	Judge	Memo		empathize
King/Queen	Juror	Message		encourage
Musical instrument	King's People	Monologue		explain
Newspaper	Musician	News story		express
Number	Newspaper	Obituary		identify
Object	Number	Owner's manual		inform
Older lady/man	Pet	Persuasive essay		investigate
Pet	Policeman/woman	Petition		persuade
Policeman/woman	Politician	Play		plagiarize
President	President	Pledge		quote
Principal	Principal	Poem		record
Rain	Sister/brother	Proposal		reflect
Science term	Science term	Reaction paper		relate
Sky	Self	Review		remark
Student	Sky/Ground	Short story		review
Teacher	Student	Skit		summarize
Tree	Teacher	Song		understand
Vehicle	TV audience	Speech		urge
Writer	Visitor	Summary		visualize

Figure 4.20
RAFT Skeleton Letter

Date _____

Dear (Audience):

First Paragraph: I am (insert Role). I am writing to you about (insert Topic). (Insert three points that you will stress in the story.)

Second Paragraph: Explain 1st point

Third Paragraph: Explain 2nd point

Fourth Paragraph: Explain 3rd point

Fifth Paragraph: Review/summarize all three points, thank the audience, and leave contact information in the event that he/she has questions.

Sincerely,

(insert Role)

11
Learn-Like-Life Activities

Provide Some Inspiration

My teacher says I'll need this stuff when I'm a little older
(I'd tell her I don't care right now if only I were bolder)
Geometry and Algebra, History, Science, English
Just how it all pertains to me I'm trying to distinguish.

Don't tell me that I'll need this when I am an adult
What you don't seem to realize is that's a blunt insult
For I'm not an adult yet and I just cannot relate
To something that has never been placed upon my plate.

So if you want my interest and my motivation
Then match it to my life today, provide some inspiration
And once I understand how I can use these things today
You won't believe the knowledge you'll be able to relay!

—Elizabeth Breaux
from *How to Reach and Teach*
ALL Students—SIMPLIFIED

What Are They?

If life is but one big classroom, why is it that in many classrooms learning is not given real-life relevance? In the real world, we all know how to teach. We teach life skills to our own children without the use of manuals, textbooks, technology, or staff development. However, when we are in our classrooms, we sometimes lose the ability to think in real-life terms! In real life our attention to certain matters is given for a variety of reasons, but seldom because it is demanded. The same applies in any classroom setting.

Charles Gibson from ABC News says that "A good reporter makes people understand how a story affects them." In other words, if it affects me I want to hear more about it. We believe that this principle holds true for good teachers as well. A good teacher makes students understand how the subject matter affects them. A good teacher entices students to engage by bridging the gap between the subject matter and the child's life. Students must believe that the subject matter being taught has relevance in their lives today.

A lesson that is relevant is creative, unique, interesting, engaging, meaningful and fun. It does not lend itself to boredom and redundancy, because in real life, things are always changing. Students must believe that the subject matter being taught in the classroom will have value outside of the classroom. Real-life teaching is, quite simply, the act of relating the subject matter to the learner's life. It is intent on creating a real-life connection, which in turn piques curiosity. It is venturing out and away from the textbook and into the real world. Bridging the gap between the subject matter and the relevance that it holds for the students, unfortunately, is where many of us fall short. Contemplate the following:

- Will memorizing historical dates in order to receive a good test score be beneficial in their lives if they do not understand how the long-term effects of those occurrences are felt today?

- Will memorizing unfamiliar words seem relevant if those words are not shown and studied in a real-life context?

- Will memorizing mathematical formulas seem pertinent if students cannot understand the significance of these formulas in the context of real-life, everyday situations?

- Will memorizing the parts of the human body (bones, organs, muscles, tendon, ligaments) have any bearing on the life of a child if he/she does not understand the awesome role that they play in maintaining their own health?

Learning in the real world is hands-on. We learn while we do. We understand when we touch and manipulate. We try, make mistakes, revamp, try again, and eventually succeed. We gain more and more knowledge of the subject matter as we continue to engage in the "doing." In the real world we intuitively understand that we must teach on the level of the learner. When we first learned to swim, for example, we were taught by someone who understood that we were non-swimmers; however there was no discussion of swimming terminology, no lecture on the mechanics of swimming, and no vocabulary assignments or worksheets given as prerequisites to the actual teaching of the skill. We eventually learned the terminology, but we learned it while we were engaging in the act of swimming. We learned and remembered because we were doing.

Classroom Scenario

Mrs. Sydney teaches reading to 25 seventh-grade students who, on any given day, seem as though they would prefer to be somewhere other than in her classroom. Many of her students are behind in attaining their reading level. Because of this, most do not enjoy reading. "They'd prefer to have a tooth pulled to reading a short story," protests Mrs. Sydney. Because student engagement is rare, Mrs. Sydney is forced to contend with the off-task behaviors that occur on a daily basis. Disciplining students has become primary to teaching. In other words, not much teaching and learning is occurring in her classroom.

"Vocabulary Day is even worse," insists Mrs. Sydney while talking to a colleague, Mr. Keith, in the lounge one day. "On an average Monday, most of them are either given punish work or sent to the office! They just will not do their work!"

Because "Vocabulary Day" was the day that students spent an entire class period copying information from a dictionary into a notebook (while the information, of course, bypassed their brains), there was no question as to why the students were engaging in more interesting pastimes. There was no question to Mr. Keith, that is. Mrs. Sydney had not yet figured it out.

"Would you say that 'Vocabulary Day' has been a virtual waste of time?" asked Mr. Keith. "The students are wasting time," admitted Mrs. Sydney before adding this question: "But how else will they read the story if they do not understand the vocabulary used in the story?" "Well," said Mr. Keith, "I'll give you a few suggestions, but first, I'd like to ask a couple of questions of you:"

1. "Is Vocabulary Day an effective use of their/your time in which effective teaching and learning are occurring? In other words, are they

learning the meaning of these unfamiliar words and how to use them in context? Do they leave your room on Mondays with a broader vocabulary base?"

2. "Is Vocabulary Day so effective that it has become the motivation for students to want to read the story? In other words, are the students anxious to read the story after 'Vocabulary Day?'"

Mrs. Sydney had to admit that learning was not occurring, and motivation to read did not exist. Unfortunately, it had not occurred to her that her "teaching" methods might be flawed. "I'm using the same teaching method that my grade-school reading teachers used. I remember many 'Vocabulary Days' and the days that followed," insisted Mrs. Sydney. "They worked just fine for me. A week looked something like this:"

1. "On Monday the teacher would place fifteen or so words on the board. We would copy the words along with their dictionary definitions into our notebooks."

2. "On Tuesday and Wednesday we would read the story."

3. "On Thursday there would be some type of review."

4. "On Thursday night one of my parents would call out the vocabulary words until I could recite each definition verbatim."

5. "On Friday I would score a 100% on the test! Wasn't that the ultimate goal?" asked Mrs. Sydney.

Mr. Keith, a veteran teacher of many years, responded in his trademark gentle tone. "It's the ultimate goal if actual 'lifelong learning' is not a goal. I'd like you to ponder a few more questions."

1. "Do you believe that you would have scored 100% on any of those tests had you been given those same tests again a month or so later?"

2. "Do you believe you were actually learning?"

3. "What if your parents had not insisted that you study… would you have learned any less? Any more?"

4. "When you read a book today, do you complete a vocabulary list before beginning? If not, how do you understand what you are reading when you encounter unfamiliar words?"

Mr. Keith had made his point. "Can you give me any suggestions?" asked Mrs. Sydney. "Better than that!" exclaimed Mr. Keith. "I'll help you to plan a lesson!"

The Differentiated Way

Planning

"Unlikely Friendships" is the premise of the story that the students will be reading. It is about a homeless man who befriends a stray cat. After discussing the story, Mr. Keith assists Mrs. Sydney in creating a list of related words that might have previously been used on a typical "Vocabulary Day." Mr. Keith suggests that a vocabulary pretest be given to all students so as to ascertain levels of knowledge before proceeding with the lesson. They devise the following list of words taken from the story:

1. shriek

2. disparage

3. exorbitant

4. timorous

5. furtive

6. itinerant

Mr. Keith assists Mrs. Sydney in preparing a simple, diagnostic pretest, to assess students' prior knowledge of the vocabulary.

NOTE: This pretest should be given a few days (possibly the week before) to the students, since the results will drive the lesson preparation.

Mr. Keith asks a few questions of Mrs. Sydney. First, he asks if she could recall any personal experiences that might be relative to the one in the text, suggesting that she could tell her own personal story as the introduction to the lesson. After giving it some thought, Mrs. Sydney remembers the time when she, a young child, had rescued a kitten.

- She remembers hearing the screeching cry, as she rode her bike home from school on one frigid winter afternoon.
- She remembers following the cry which led her to a tree where she found the kitten stranded in the upper branches.
- She remembers climbing halfway up the tree and then coaxing the kitten downward.
- She remembers that the kitten fell and that she thought the kitten could not have survived it. She remembers it lying in the tall grass, shaking the hard fall from its body, and running toward her.
- She remembers how frail and needy the kitten had appeared.

- She remembers the kitten clinging to her and crying frantically when she placed it back on the ground.

- She remembers the dilemma: How would she take care of this kitten when her parents had already insisted that the family not have any pets?

- She remembers arriving home and hiding it in her book sack while she prepared a bowl of bread and milk.

- She remembers the gentle purring as the kitten nuzzled her neck and slept so peacefully.

- She remembers the name that she gave to him: *Lucky*. And she remembers how unlucky she felt when her father first saw the kitten, took it from her grasp, and left the room....

As Mrs. Sydney spoke of that day almost twenty years ago, tears filled Mr. Keith's eyes. "Do you have any idea what you have just done?" asked Mr. Keith. "I cannot wait to hear more! And if the story in the text is similar, I am anxious to read it! What happened after your father left with the kitten?" Mrs. Sydney continued to share her recollections.

- "I remember crying hysterically into my pillow, not knowing what my father might do, but assuming that whatever it was, it would not be good."

- "I remember riding my bike to school the next morning, passing that tree, and secretly wishing that the kitten would be there once again, stranded and waiting to be rescued. This time I would hide him well. I would care for him well. And I would love him better than anyone else possibly could. No one, not even my father, would take him away."

- "I remember arriving home and not wanting to enter the house. I remember the pain turning to anger toward my father. I remember the scene in the kitchen as I walked in. My father was holding the kitten while my mother filled a bowl with food. I saw the tag that hung around Lucky's neck. I knew he was there to stay for a long time."

Mrs. Sydney finished the story. As it turned out, her father had taken the kitten to the veterinarian to have it examined. Not knowing whether or not it was healthy, he had not wanted to give his daughter any false hope in regard to the kitten becoming part of the family.

"For how long was he a part of your family?" asked Mr. Keith, "Almost sixteen years," replied Mrs. Sydney, with tears in her eyes. "And I remember his final day as the second most 'lucky' one in his life. It was the day that I, a first-year teacher, only 23 years old, chose to help him to end it. Lucky had become ill, diagnosed with cancer. I chose to help him to end his suffering. It was the most peaceful thing I have ever seen; except for that peaceful purring I can still remember from the day that I, an eight-year-old child, rescued him from the tree."

"OK," said Mr. Keith, "You've got me now! And you will have hooked the students too after a story like that."

Mr. Keith suggests that Mrs. Sydney plan time for allowing students to ask questions and to share their own personal stories. He also suggests that she follow this storytelling session with a story-writing session where the students are given time to put their personal stories into writing. He advises her to collect the stories. He suggests that after Mrs. Sydney and her students finish sharing and writing their own stories, they begin reading the assigned story together. He proposes that Mrs. Sydney plan to actually read the first couple of paragraphs of the story to the students and then ask a few relevant questions at various levels of thinking. Questions should be prepared for use at key points throughout the story.

NOTE: Specific questions should be prepared for specific students, with individual needs in mind. When preparing these individual questions, refer to the students' personal stories. Tailor the questions so that they relate to each individual. This will keep the lesson "real-life" in nature and assist in keeping students engaged.

Mr. Keith recommends that Mrs. Sydney incorporate a hands-on vocabulary activity to be used as the unfamiliar words are encountered while reading, as opposed to beforehand as had been done on previous "Vocabulary Days." Mrs. Sydney prepares 25 identical activity bags (zippered bags), one for each student, each containing 18 strips upon which the following are written:

1. Six strips with one vocabulary word each printed upon it.

2. Six strips with one definition each printed upon it.

3. Six strips with one sentence each printed upon it. Each sentence contains a blank space where the proper vocabulary word will be inserted.

NOTE: Don't forget to laminate everything! The time-consuming preparation work should be done only once. Just store and file away for upcoming years!

"And don't forget to continue using the words, as much as you possibly can during the reading of the story," said Mr. Keith. "Keep coming back to them. Use them over and over in context. Once the reading of the story has been completed, have students empty the entire bag of 18 strips and attempt to put together all at once. Prepare additional bags with additional sentences. Allow students to attempt to fill in those blanks with the six words. Write the words on the board, on your word wall, on your own forehead! Ask your team of teachers to use the words in their room that week as much as possible. Then, give a vocabulary test at the end of the lesson. You and your students will be amazed at how well they will do, and without studying/memorizing anything! This will help you to prove to yourself and to your students that true learning has occurred!"

Let's take a look at the manner in which this lesson should progress:

1. A vocabulary pretest will be given in advance.

2. Mrs. Sydney will tell a personal story and allow students to share their personal stories.

3. Mrs. Sydney will instruct her students to put their personal stories into writing.

4. Questions will be asked at key points throughout the assigned story. Specific questions will be asked to specific students based on individual differences. All questions will include references to each student's personal story.

5. Hands-on vocabulary development activities will be used as unfamiliar words are encountered while reading.

6. A post-test will be given as a culmination of the lesson.

Mrs. Sydney administered the vocabulary pretest on the previous Friday. The results were as expected; few students had any previous knowledge of the vocabulary. Because of that, she prepared the activity bags so that, at first, all students would receive the same materials.

NOTE: She prepared additional bags for those who might grasp the meanings more quickly. The additional bags included activities involving word origin, extended meaning, and unfamiliar words with similar meanings.

Implementation

Mrs. Sydney didn't waste any time starting the lesson. When the bell rang on Monday morning, Mrs. Sydney stood in front of her students, many of whom had already prepared their notebooks for "Vocabulary Day," and asked that they clear their desks. "We are skipping 'Vocabulary Day' this week," she announced as the class applauded! "Instead, I would like to begin by sharing a personal story with you. It is one that I have not often told, but it is nevertheless quite worth recounting. It is one that makes me both happy and sad, so I will probably become a little emotional while telling it. I know you will all understand why once I have finished sharing it with you." The students' eyes are on Mrs. Sydney as she proceeds to relate the experience that began many years ago.

As was expected, the students were mesmerized by the story and had many questions to ask and stories of their own to share. After proclaiming her love for each student's own story, she asked that they put them into writing. She used these personal stories to create individual questions to be asked at key points throughout the reading of the story.

The next day, Mrs. Sydney proceeded to tell them a little about the story in the text that they would read next. She told them just enough to pique their curiosities. She explained that it bore a close resemblance to the story she had shared on the previous day.

She began by reading the first page to the students, after which she asked that they put their books aside. She proceeded to ask questions. Since the questions had been previously prepared and the names of specific students denoted next to each question, the process was quite easily implemented and highly effective.

Mrs. Sydney wrote the word *timorous* on the board and asked if anyone could define the word. Some tried, but none could. "We are about to come upon this word on the next page. Let's see if the meaning becomes a little clearer when used in a sentence." She continued to read, stopping after the word was encountered in context. "At first, the stray kitten appeared *timorous*, hiding behind the lamppost and crouching closely to the ground." Mrs. Sydney stopped and distributed activity bags. She instructed students to pull out all 18 strips and to divide the strips into three separate stacks, each stack to include the following:

1. Stack #1: vocabulary words

2. Stack #2: definitions of words

3. Stack #3: sentences with blank spaces.

She instructed students to pull the word *timorous* from the vocabulary stack. She shared a few more sentences that used the word in context. "Now go to your definition stack and attempt to find the correct definition of *timorous*," she said. She monitored the students so as to informally assess their levels of understanding. A discussion was held, questions were answered, and the correct definition was agreed upon. "Go to your sentence stack," she said, "and try to find the sentence where the word *timorous* would be most appropriately used." Again, she informally assessed through monitoring and providing a question/answer period. The word *timorous* was then placed upon the word wall, and the class resumed the reading of the story.

This process continued throughout the reading of the story. To students who were able to readily determine word meaning used in context, the additional bags with activities involving word origin, extended meanings, and unfamiliar words with similar meanings, were administered. All words were placed upon the wall and used repeatedly throughout the week.

Upon completion of the story, students were given an unannounced post-test. All exceeded the levels at which they had previously been performing, yet none had "studied" the content in preparation for the test. Mrs. Sydney had proven to herself the point that Mr. Keith had intended: real-life, hands-on teaching provides students with the skills to become lifelong learners.

Variations

- Math: Teach in real-life settings so that students understand the relevance and appreciate the material's real-life application. We teach these formulas so that students can apply them throughout their lives in real-world situations, so why would we teach outside of that context in the classroom?
- History: Avoid teaching facts without relating them to the effects that they have on students' lives today. A mind full of facts is meaningless if their uses seem impractical in real-life endeavors.
- Physical Education: Avoid the over-teaching of team sports and focus more on the body, its functions and abilities, and our personal responsibilities in caring for and creating a fit body whose parts work in perfect conjunction with one another. Teach socialization and problem-solving skills as part of teamwork, and you may discover that more students will become more interested in team sports after all.

The Bottom Line

Real life is "hands-on"; we learn by doing. We improve with practice, but true learning is forever. In real life, we engage when we become interested and when we can see the relevance that concepts have in our own lives. Real-life teaching brings the real world into the classroom. Isn't that where it has belonged all along?

12
Team Teaching

Teamwork

If two heads are better than one
Then three should be better by far
For one all alone must rely on himself
While the team works at raising the bar.

The loner works fine in some circles
But others require that the load
Be carried by several, all working together
As one traveling down the same road.

Players must count on the squad
While members depend on the band
Actors rest on the cast for support
And contestants need audience hands.

Teachers need help from each other
And students must trust that the team
Is working together on every endeavor
And sutured at every seam.

—Elizabeth Breaux

What Is It?

Team Teaching is not a new concept, yet it is one that is often underutilized. When employed in a carefully calculated, well-planned manner, it can be invaluable. When teachers, facilitators, teacher assistants, adult tutors, administrators, volunteers, etc., teach as one unit, accomplishments can be monumental. This too, of course, takes concerted planning, but the rewards can be innumerable.

For proper execution to occur, teachers must be willing to work together as one team for the benefit of the students. Teachers must be willing to put aside differences so that student achievement can be the primary focus.

If properly executed, Team Teaching can easily accommodate individual differences. When logistics are structured to accommodate individual needs, the activities and assessments can be tailored to meet those differences.

Team Teaching can take a variety of forms:

1. In a true "Teaming" school, teams of teachers (possibly three-to-five per team) are given one large group of students (75–125 or so per team). Classes move as units from one teacher to another. The advantage is that all teachers teach all students on the team. Scheduling affords these teams of teachers common planning time, which can be used for:

    * planning cross-curricular lessons.

    * planning more unconventional types of lessons where student movement might be driven by necessity as opposed to bells.

    * planning for more individualized instruction where students might be regrouped according to readiness levels in regard to subject matter.

    * discussing individual needs of particular students.

    * meetings with parents (where parents meet with all of their child's teachers at one time).

    * meetings with individual students.

    * planning for remediation and/or enrichment activities.

2. Non-teaming schools require more creative effort on the parts of the teachers, but coming together as a team can still be accomplished (see "Variations" p. 159).

Classroom Scenario

The sixth-grade teachers at Marshall Middle School incorporate Team Teaching to perfection. They rarely plan lessons in isolation, choosing instead to teach using a true cross-curricular concept. At the beginning of each six-week period, they meet at length and plan for the upcoming weeks. During the teaching phase they maintain contact with one another. They have agreed that flexibility is the key, and that regardless of their own personal differences, opinions, work ethics, etc., they will do whatever it takes as long as it is in the best interest of the students. They epitomize the adage *"Children First."*

NOTE: It is important to note that this is not a "Teaming" school. Common planning time is not built into the daily schedule.

The Differentiated Way

Planning

The four teachers met on the Friday afternoon preceding the start of a new six-week period. During the meeting, they discussed their individual grade-level expectations for the upcoming six-week period, and recorded all information onto a chart that would serve as a very broad, basic, simplified overview of their teaching and learning expectations for the upcoming grading period (see figure 4.21, p. 161). While constructing the chart, they discussed their individual goals and objectives and brainstormed ways to correlate those with one another into their individual disciplines so that true cross-curricular teaching could occur. Each teacher left the meeting with a copy of the overview chart, which they intended to use as a reference when planning upcoming lessons.

Each teacher trusts that the others will find ways to connect their curriculum to their own. If all teachers vow to do this, instruction in one class will be reinforced in other classrooms throughout the day. Because the teachers have developed very positive, open working relationships, they feel comfortable asking for suggestions from one another as time progresses.

Implementation

Let's use Week 4 (see figure 4.21, p. 161) as an example of how the four teachers were able to correlate their lessons. During Week 4, the following Grade-Level Expectations were dictated to the teachers via the state curriculum guide (*samples taken from the Louisiana Comprehensive Curriculum for Sixth-Grade*). Teachers were expected to address these as required, but the activities could be tailored as deemed necessary by each teacher.

Teacher/Subject Area	Week 4
Mrs. Shadden/ *English-Language Arts*	Compare and contrast cultural characteristics (e.g., customs, traditions, viewpoints) found in national, world, and multicultural literature.
Mrs. Hayes/ *Math*	Describe and analyze trends and patterns.
Ms. Rees/ *Science*	Compare physical and chemical changes.
Mr. Brown/ *Social Studies*	Explain reasons for different patterns of migration among early peoples.

The teachers noticed that a common thread/theme could be detected in the expectations in week 4, so they used that to guide their lessons. The four teachers determined that the concepts of *Comparison, Analysis, and Patterns* could be interwoven into all disciplines that week. Because all of them were experts in their own areas, they needed to acquire some information from one another, which is what all teachers who work as a team must do.

- Mrs. Shadden, the English/language arts teacher, discussed the application of trends and patterns in a math environment with the math teacher, Mrs. Hayes, for verification purposes.
- Ms. Rees, the science teacher, consulted with Mr. Brown, the social studies teacher, as to how she could use the concept of patterns when teaching students about physical and chemical changes in various substances.
- Mrs. Hayes, the math teacher, immediately saw the opportunity to incorporate the patterns of migration from Mr. Brown's social studies lesson into her instruction on analyzing trends and patterns.
- Mr. Brown and Mrs. Shadden, the social studies and English/language arts teachers, were excited about how closely related their topics of study would be, so they planned together on most days during the grading period.

Let's take a closer look into the classrooms of each teacher during week 4.

1. **English/Language Arts (Mrs. Shadden):**
   - In reference to *trends and patterns* being studied in math class, she incorporated the two terms into her discussions on *cultural characteristics found in literature*. Students were then divided into randomly selected groups where they rotated through several Centers. At each center students used sets of manipulatives to find trends and patterns in previously read literature.
   - She compared the *cultural characteristics of literature* from various periods to the *physical changes* being discussed in science class.
   - She showed how the *patterns of migration* that were being studied in social studies affected *cultural characteristics,* which in turn influenced certain pieces of literature.
   - At the end of the six-week period, Mrs. Shadden created a Connect Four activity (see Chapter 4, #9) with critical thinking questions that incorporated all four disciplines. To complete the Connect Four questions, students used knowledge from all areas of study.

2. **Math (Mrs. Hayes):**
   - Mrs. Hayes decided to use the strategy of Tiered Assignments (see Chapter 4, #4) once she was able to determine readiness levels and levels of understanding of the topic.

       1. She divided her students into four distinct groups: high, medium-high, medium-low, and low.

       2. She created assignments at varying levels of difficulty so as to accommodate each group.

       3. All assignments were based on *trends and patterns*, but she incorporated topics being studied in the other disciplines.

   - When analyzing mathematical *trends and patterns*, Mrs. Hayes compared them to *trends in cultural characteristics found in literature,* as was being studied in English/language arts class.
   - When discussing *trends and patterns* in a mathematical format, she made reference to the *trends and patterns of migration among early peoples,* as was being studied in social studies class.

- She compared the *trends and patterns* found in scientific physical compositions to those found in mathematical formulas.

4. **Science (Ms. Rees):**

   - Ms. Rees had her students use the RAFT writing format (see Chapter 4, #10) to associate *physical changes in substances* and *physical changes that occurred when land features were changed by early migrators.*

Role:	Physically changed plot of land
Audience:	Early people
Format:	Speech
Topic:	Effects of destroying trees

   - Ms. Rees required her students to complete a project where differences in *physical features of people* of different cultures were compared to differences in *physical characteristics of certain substances.*

   - When performing an experiment on the *chemical changes* of certain substances, Ms. Rees' students were asked to list the *patterns and trends* found in the process as it related to all of the substances.

5. **Social Studies (Mr. Brown):**

   - Mr. Brown used the Jigsaw Puzzles strategy (see Chapter 4, #2) as an opener to the unit on patterns of migration of early peoples. The topic of study was divided into four sub-topics or "pieces":

     1. climate and terrain

     2. disease

     3. shelter

     4. food and water

   Students were grouped according to Multiple Intelligences.

   - Mr. Brown had his students create charts detailing the *patterns of migration of people of different cultures.* He gave the charts to the math teacher to use as an analogy when discussing *trends and patterns in mathematical formulas.*

- Mr. Brown sought advice form Mrs. Shadden, the English/language arts teacher, as to which literature pieces he could use as part of his lesson that would help to reinforce the *effects of migration among early peoples*.
- Mr. Brown's students completed a project where they built a model of an early settlement. The model was to show how the *patterns of migration* being studied influenced *physical changes* (studied in science class) in the lands.

Variations

- Two eleventh-grade math teachers teach a real-life lesson outdoors, together, to both classes at once. Both teachers are there to teach, assist, give individualized attention, assess, etc.
- Two special education teachers, along with their teacher assistants, take students to a museum. Students are divided into four groups. Each group visits a different area of the museum. All come together and share experiences.
- Three seventh-grade alternative education classes are restructured by the teachers. After several weeks of getting to know the students, the three teachers come together and create three new groups/classes: low, average, and above average. Since these three groups rotate among the three teachers (language arts, social studies/science, and math), teachers are able to create lessons that better meet the needs of each individual group.
- A first-grade teacher uses her parent/grandparent volunteers on a rotating basis. They monitor and give assistance as needed. They are able to assist in keeping students on task as well as assisting students who are struggling with new concepts/ideas.
- An eighth-grade inclusion class consists of 22 regular education students and 7 special education students. The regular and special education teacher teach together on a daily basis. Because the special education teacher has been given a teacher assistant, there are three adults in the room at all times. The teachers often plan lessons where Centers are used. Each adult is responsible for overseeing a particular center. For example, at one center guided reading might take place, while at another center the students work using technology. At the third center a hands-on activity involving story elements might occur. Groups move from center to center with the guidance and assistance of the three adults.

The Bottom Line

Team Teaching, no matter what form it takes, is always a team effort. A team is only as effective as its individual members; thus, it is critical that all members develop good working relationships. Teaching in isolation removes the potential for the sharing of ideas, strategies, new activities, etc. Use one another, share with one another, plan with one another, and develop a team that ensures that its players, the students, achieve success.

Figure 4.21
Grade Level Expectations

These are samples of Grade Level Expectations for sixth grade taken from the Louisiana Comprehensive Curriculum.

	Sample Week 1	Sample Week 2	Sample Week 3	Sample Week 4	Sample Week 5	Sample Week 6
Mrs. Shadden *English/LanguageArts*	Identify and explain story elements, including: theme development, character development, word choice, mood	Identify and explain story elements, including: plot sequence (e.g., exposition, rising action, climax, falling action, resolution)	Identify and explain literary and sound devices, including: Foreshadowing, flashback, imagery, onomatopoeia	Compare and contrast cultural characteristics (e.g., customs, traditions, viewpoints) found in national, world, and multicultural literature	Classify and interpret elements of various genres: Fiction: myth, historical fiction Non-fiction: article	Classify and interpret elements of various genres: Poetry, drama
Mrs. Hayes *Math*	Interpret data from tables	Calculate mean, median, and mode	Solve counting logic problems	Describe and analyze trends and patterns	Apply concept of complementary events	Decipher data from tables, lists, diagrams, etc.
Ms. Rees *Science*	Measure and record the volume and mass of substances in metric system units	Calculate the density of large and small quantities of a variety of substances	Differentiate between the physical and chemical properties of selected substances	Compare physical and chemical changes	Identify the average atomic masses of given elements using the periodic table	Use a variety of resources to identify elements and compounds in common substances
Mr. Brown *Social Studies*	Use latitude and longitude to determine direction or locate or compare points on a map or representation of a globe	Identify land and climatic conditions conducive to human settlement and describe the role of these conditions	Identify physical features that influenced world historical events and describe their influence	Explain reasons for different patterns of migration among early peoples	Describe the economic interdependence among various ancient civilizations	Explain how ancient civilizations established and maintained political boundaries

Conclusion

When the ending lines are spoken
When the credits all have run
When my numbered days uncoil into
Their one last setting sun
When the closing curtain frees its folds
And the final call is made
I'll exit proudly and with no regrets
My teacher's stage.

—Elizabeth Breaux

Teachers—

Nothing mentioned in this book is easy, but we knew when we first signed up to become teachers that nothing in this profession would ever be easy. We became teachers because we wanted to influence students and make a difference in their lives. That, itself, is a formidable task.

It is because we love children that we have chosen to devote our lives to them. We must never take that mission lightly. In our endeavor, we must always treat each child as a worthy, unique individual, with as much promise as the next. Again, this is an awesome task...but who better to undertake it than us, the teachers?

Our hope for you and for your students is that you can create for them the ultimate learning environment, wrought with possibilities, and that you and they can enjoy and remember fondly every minute of the process.

We are the teachers. We are the ones who shape lives. We are the ones who fashion futures...

...and we are the ones who matter most. For without us, there is nothing...

Best regards,

Liz Breaux and
Monique Boutte Magee

References

Breaux, Annette and Elizabeth, (2003) *Real Teachers, Real Challenges, Real Solutions*. Larchmont, NY: Eye on Education.

Breaux, Elizabeth, (2005) *Classroom Management—SIMPLIFIED*. Larchmont, NY: Eye on Education.

Breaux, Elizabeth, (2007) *How to Reach and Teach ALL Students—SIMPLIFIED*. Larchmont, NY: Eye on Education.

Breaux, Elizabeth, (2008) *How the BEST TEACHERS Avoid the 20 Most Common Teaching Mistakes*. Larchmont, NY: Eye on Education.

Dalton, J. & Smith, D., (1986) Extending Children's Special Abilities – Strategies for primary classrooms.

Fleming, Grace n.d. Learning Styles Retrieved from: homeworktips.about.com/od/homeworkhelp/a/learningstyle.htm July 2009

Gardner, Howard, (2006) *Multiple Intelligences New Horizons*. New York: Basic Books.

Giles, Emily, Pitre, Sarah, & Womack, Sara. n.d. Multiple Intelligences and Learning Styles Retrieved from: http://projects.coe.uga.edu/epltt/index.php?title=Multiple_Intelligences_and_Learning_Styles July 2009.

Graves, Terra n.d. Writing Across the Curriculum Retrieved from: www.writingfix.com June 2009.

Gregory, Gayle, (2008) *Differentiated Instructional Strategies in Practice*. Thousand Oaks, CA: Corwin Press.

Gregory, Gayle, (2008) *Differentiated Instructional Strategies for Science*. Thousand Oaks, CA: Corwin Press.

Jester, Catherine n.d. A Learning Style Survey for College Retrieved from: www.metamath.com/multiple/multiple_choice_questions.html July 2009.

Johnson, Roger T. & David n.d. An Overview of Cooperative Learning. Retrieved from: http://www.co-operation.org/pages/overviewpaper.html June 2009.

Louisiana Comprehensive Curriculum. n.d. Retrieved from: http://www.doe.state.la.us/lde/saa/2108.html June 2009.

Mantle, Stacy, (2001) The Seven Learning Styles Retrieved from: www.lessontutor.com/sm1.html June 2009.

McKenzie, Walter, (1999) Multiple Intelligences Inventory Retrieved from: http://surfaquarium.com/MI/inventory.htm.

Northwest Regional Education Laboratory, n.d. Designing R.A.F.T.S Writing Assignments Retrieved from: http://doe.sd.gov/curriculum/6plus1/docs/educators/docs/RAFTS.pdf June 2009

Reis. S, Burns, D.E. Renzulli, J.S., (1992) Curriculum Compacting: The complete guide to modifying the regular curriculum for high ability students.

Siegle, Del, (1999) Curriculum Compacting: A Necessity for Academic Advancement Retrieved from: http://www.gifted.uconn.edu/nrcgt/newsletter/fall99/fall996.html June 2009.

Stahl, Robert, (1994) The Essential Elements of Cooperative Learning in the Classroom Retrieved from: ERIC Digest www.ericdigests.org/1995-1/elements.htm July 2009.

Tillman, Marianne, (2003) Differentiated Instruction Retrieved from: www.3villagecsd.k12.ny.us/Instructional_Technology/TchLrn/Differentinstructoverview.htm June 2009.

Tomlinson, Carol, (2001) *How to Differentiate Instruction in Mixed Ability Classrooms*. Alexandria, VA: Association for Supervision & Curriculum Development.

Tomlinson, Carol, (2000) *Leadership for Differentiating Schools and Classrooms*. Alexandria, VA: Association for Supervision & Curriculum Development.

Tomlinson, Carol, (1999) *The Differentiated Classroom: Responding to the Needs of All Learners*. Alexandria, VA: Association for Supervision & Curriculum Development.

Williams, Bruce, (2002) *Multiple Intelligences For Differentiated Learning*. Thousand Oaks, CA: Corwin Press.

Elizabeth Breaux is an international speaker and presenter.
If you would like information on inviting her
to speak to your faculty or group,
please contact her at

www.educationspeakersgroup.com
or
lizooofarms@cox.net
or
(337-654-0040)